Lucy Carr.

MODERN POETS FIVE

MODERN POETS FIVE

Edited by
JIM HUNTER

Headmaster, Weymouth Grammar School

FABER AND FABER
London   Boston

First published in 1981
by Faber and Faber Limited
3 Queen Square London WC1N 3AU
Printed in Great Britain by
Latimer Trend & Company Ltd Plymouth
All rights reserved

This selection © Faber and Faber Limited 1981

British Library Cataloguing in Publication Data

Modern Poets.
  5
  1. English poetry – 20th century
  I. Hunter, Jim
  821'.9'1208   PR1225

ISBN 0-571-11567-5

CONTENTS

INTRODUCTION

This anthology is a sequel to a four-volume collection, MODERN POETS, first published in 1968 (the last volume has since been revised). The principle behind that selection was: 'Here are some poets that deserve our attention', rather than a dogmatic claim to have found 'the best'. And the idea was to have relatively few poets, well represented. So inevitably many famous and good writers were left out, and the choice became harder the nearer to our own time it got.

MODERN POETS FIVE is similarly selected, and presents poets who have become known in the 1970s. I took the decision to leapfrog over scores of good poets of the fifties and sixties (rather as I did in 1968 with Seamus Heaney). It seems to me important that the young readers for whom this collection is primarily intended should meet some very recent writing, particularly when it is so good and so accessible. So, with the striking and unusual exception of C. H. Sisson, who first really found his voice in middle age, all the poets here are younger than Seamus Heaney, and have, I hope, as Heaney himself probably does, a lot of writing ahead of them. And, I repeat, I don't claim they are 'the best'; only that they are good, I like them, and I think they are rewarding to study.

Poetry is very much alive in Britain. Attractively produced paperbacks of new poets' work are now standard, and we should be grateful to a number of editors and publishers, even if a dark suspicion lurks at times that graceful, competent work is keeping out bolder experimental writing. Restraint and technical efficiency are normal; so is the appearance of form, even when the form itself is hard to pin down. Fairly often in the twentieth century, especially in

America, it looked as if the verse-line as a unit had been virtually dismembered: in the anxiety to capture speech rhythm, the idea of poetic rhythm seemed almost to get lost. That has all changed; all the poets in this volume write fine verse, and some of my notes try to point this out—not in order to be 'academic', but because the choice of medium is vital in art, and the poets know that. Most of these poems ask to be spoken aloud, and I hope the book will enable them to figure in a good many poetry-readings in the next few years.

As for the 'restraint': at its best it is not modesty (a questionable virtue) but a pursuit of integrity. This is clearest in Sisson and Paulin, but characteristic of the others too—Andrew Motion's perilously meticulous ANNIVER-SARIES, or his similar care not to dramatize his visit to Anne Frank's house; Waterman's GARDENS; Wells reaching time and again for calm but not for false ease; and Craig Raine in the mortuary, accepting clear-eyed the 'unacceptable' comparisons ('two terra cotta nipples/like patches from a cycle kit,/puzzled knees . . .') because they seem right and true. Whatever the state of Britain's economy (or, one might add, its fiction), if we have poetry so technically poised and so steadily seeking integrity, we may be glad to be here.

In preparing the book, I have several times asked a poet to clarify for me a particular phrase or reference. The notes, though, are truly mine, and my fault. I am grateful to a number of friends for conversation and information, among them John Adams, Ruth and Richard Blake, John Laver, Charles Monteith, Geoff Pawling and Mike Perrin.

JIM HUNTER

C. H. Sisson

C. H. Sisson was born in Bristol in 1914. He read English at the University of Bristol and later also studied in Germany and France. From 1936 until his retirement he worked in the Civil Service, apart from a three-year period in the Forces during the Second World War. He started writing poetry relatively late, but has become in the last ten years a newly known poet and a significant influence on writers many years younger.

Sisson's viewpoint is, in a rather bleak way, Christian, classicist, and conservative if not reactionary. A general distrust of human institutions and human vanities (he was a sharp critic of the Civil Service from within) is extended most acutely to himself—or, perhaps one should say, to the 'I' speakers of his poems. In the brief foreword to his Collected Poems (IN THE TROJAN DITCH) he speaks of having recourse to translation, as a way of writing without indulging in self-gratification or self-importance. 'I have come in the end to have great sympathy with Dryden, who having pushed his way this way and that at the end of his days took pride in being able to do a translation better than any of them. He was glad, I imagine, to be able to release the energies of poetry without passing for having said anything of his own.'

The dourness of Sisson's judgements of himself and man is not a lack of sensitivity. Pain, the possibilities of at least transitory delight, and a latent compassion make a tense life under the dry surface. Occasionally harshness and scepticism fall silent in a calm rural landscape; and behind all is God, 'the only friend'. In literary terms Sisson tries to keep free of influences and go for the speaking voice, though we may feel some echoes of Eliot, the leading poet for Sisson's generation.

The strongest real source for Sisson is Latin poetry, with its slightly metallic and ironic lyricism and its sardonic struggles with sexual warmth and sexual disgust. A reader eager to understand Sisson closely will want to know at least a translation (perhaps Sisson's own) of the poems of Catullus, and attend particularly to the poem CATULLUS in this selection, which indicates something of Sisson's religious thinking however controversial its view of Catullus himself.

'When I did the Catullus,' Sisson says—referring to his translation—'the exercise in plainness was what I wanted.' This is one reason why Sisson is valued by younger poets in England today: plainness is seen as a way to integrity. As another clue to Sisson's intentions, his comment on translating Virgil is equally helpful: in Virgil, 'there is a certain elaboration, very unfashionable in our time and perhaps of little use for contemporary literary purposes. There is also something which we ought to value. This is a deep movement of feeling, below the surface of our exacerbated daily life, and which has greater significance than any "frankness" for those who want to understand the human brute.'

Ellick Farm

The larks flew up like jack-in-the-boxes
From my moors, and the fields were edged with
                                    foxgloves.
The farm lay neatly within the hollow
The gables climbing, the barn beside the doorway.

If I had climbed into the loft I should have found a
                                    boy
Forty years back, among the bales of hay.

He would have known certainly all that I know
Seeing it in the muck-strewn cobbles below.

(Under the dark rim of the near wood
The tears gathered as under an eyelid.)

It would have surprised him to see a tall man
Who had travelled far, pretending to be him.

But that he should have been turning verses, half dumb
After half a lifetime, would least have surprised him.

The Temple

Who are they talking to in the big temple?
If there were a reply it would be a conversation:
It is because there is none that they are fascinated.
What does not reply is the answer to prayer.

Easter

One good crucifixion and he rose from the dead
He knew better than to wait for age
To nibble his intellect
And depress his love.

Out in the desert the sun beats and the cactus
Prickles more fiercely than any in his wilderness
And his forty days
Were merely monastic.

What he did on the cross was no more
Than others have done for less reason
And the resurrection you could take for granted.

What is astonishing is that he came here at all
Where no one ever came voluntarily before.

A and B

A.
I was in the lane and saw the car pass.
The white face of the girl showed through the
                                        windscreen,
Beside her a youth with a tight grip on the wheel.

B.
There was a blue Anglia; I remember.

A.
I caught the girl's eyes as she passed;
They were in deepest contentment.
She communicated in perfect freedom to me
The candour with which she would undress when they
                                        reached the wood.
It was a point that had been troubling the boy.

B.
And what has their pleasure to do with us?

A.
You think a philosopher should stick to his port.
That is not my opinion.
What is enacted in these hills
Is a sacrifice as any propounded
Under the shadow of the Giant of Cerne
And sacrifice is not for the actors.

B.
What nonsense is this about a sacrifice?
This is what two people did, and that is all.

A.

What they did in a flurry of consciousness,
Their hands upon one another's sides,
Was trivial enough. But what were their intentions?
Some hope perhaps of giving or taking pleasure.

B.

I should think they might have been partially
            successful.

A.

I met an old man on a tall horse
He had ridden for thirty years. It was his intention
When he had seen the last of it, to bury it
Out in that field beside his dead mare.
Do you think he had planned that harmony?
Did not a spirit seize him by the throat
And tell him what to do: there, under the old church
Rising there on that mound above the groin?

B.

I am afraid, A, you are not a philosopher.
You are merely an inconsiderate fool who loves his
              country
At the very moment when love has become vain.

A.

See there where a party of picnickers
Trace their way over the springy turf
And the world proceeds without understanding.
Perhaps all will be well.

A Letter to John Donne

Note: On 27 July 1617, Donne preached at the parish church at Sevenoaks, of which he was rector, and was entertained at Knole, then the country residence of Richard Sackville, third earl of Dorset.

I understand you well enough, John Donne
First, that you were a man of ability
Eaten by lust and by the love of God
Then, that you crossed the Sevenoaks High Street
As rector of Saint Nicholas:
I am of that parish.

To be a man of ability is not much
You may see them on the Sevenoaks platform any day
Eager men with despatch cases
Whom ambition drives as they drive the machine
Whom the certainty of meticulous operation
Pleasures as a morbid sex a heart of stone.

That you could have spent your time in the corruption
                         of courts
As these in that of cities, gives you no place among us:
Ability is not even the game of a fool
But the click of a computer operating in a waste
Your cleverness is dismissed from this suit
Bring out your genitals and your theology.

What makes you familiar is this dual obsession;
Lust is not what the rutting stag knows
It is to take Eve's apple and to lose
The stag's paradisal look:
The love of God comes readily
To those who have most need.

You brought body and soul to this church
Walking there through the park alive with deer
But now what animal has climbed into your pulpit?
One whose pretension is that the fear
Of God has heated him into a spirit
An evaporated man no physical ill can hurt.

Well might you hesitate at the Latin gate
Seeing such apes denying the church of God:
I am grateful particularly that you were not a saint
But extravagant whether in bed or in your shroud.
You would understand that in the presence of folly
I am not sanctified but angry.

Come down and speak to the men of ability
On the Sevenoaks platform and tell them
That at your Saint Nicholas the faith
Is not exclusive in the fools it chooses
That the vain, the ambitious and the highly sexed
Are the natural prey of the incarnate Christ.

Catullus

Catullus walked in the Campus Martius.
He had seen all he needed to see,
Lain on his bed at noon, and got up to his whore.
His heart had been driven out of his side
By a young bitch—well, she was beautiful,
Even, while the illusion was with him, tender.
She had resolved herself into splayed legs
And lubricity in the most popular places.

He had seen Caesar who—had he not been, once,
The drunken pathic of the King of Bithynia?—
Returning in triumph from the western isles:
Nothing was too good for this unique emperor.
Against these fortunes he had nothing to offer
—Possibly the remains of his indignation,
A few verses that would outlive the century.
His mind was a clear lake in which he had swum:
There was nothing but to await a new cloud.
We have seen it. But Catullus did not;
He had already hovered his thirty years
On the edge of the Mediterranean basin.
The other, rising like a whirlwind in a remote province,
Was of a character he would have ignored.
And yet the body burnt out by lechery,
Turning to its tomb, was awaiting this,
Forerunning as surely as John the Baptist
An impossible love pincered from a human form.

VALEDICTION

Catullus my friend across twenty centuries,
Anxious to complete your lechery before Christ came.

Stanza

Every year blackthorn and daffodil
Are noticed by those who imagine they are renewed
When the year is. But they grow old,
The renewal of hope is vain: it is their grandchildren
Who come laughing along the road, picking the
                                        cowslips.

Adam

I will go and visit the deer
They and the cat being my main accompaniments,
As it happens, in the silence which succeeds work.
The sunlight whitens the top of the chestnuts,
Bare for winter, and the snow
Blazes to gold. The cat is safe in the house.
Out there under the magnificent beeches
The deer have classified themselves according to sex.
Not creatures of man's invention
Still they nuzzle or walk where he has put them.
I, creature of God, am among man's artifacts.
With the beasts I creep into another day.
Nothing commands me to a particular form;
But for my name and address I might be water
Running into a puddle for the cat to lick
Or perhaps stretching its ripples in the sunlight
Among the frosted grass, for the deer to stale.
I acknowledge freely that I am part of the creation
But doubt whether I am a particle for whom salvation
                        was intended.
My sympathy is with Adam
Walking in the garden in the cool of the day.
To avoid is best.

ADAM: But that was in fact not exactly my problem.
Like you of course I admitted I was created
—In my case it was self-evident;
God was always about like the breath of my nostrils.
Moreover I was, next him, the lord of the garden
And had given names to the animals one by one

As he presented them to me. It was because none of
                                   these
Seemed more than a rustle of the grasses through
                            which they came
That I was presented with Eve. And I was astonished.
There was a new element of correspondence
Not perceptible then in the beasts, though now you
                                   see it.
The foolishness of the apron of fig-leaves
Was a first effort to rid myself of that.
When God called there was some confusion.
It was the first time he had spoken so loudly.
I thought he was another kind of Eve,
A more powerful Adam perhaps, like myself.
The conversation that followed was hallucinatory.
It is easy for you to laugh at our evasions.
The future was unsettled.
I decided to walk out of Eden and go to work.
Since then nothing has been clear.
If I see Paradise it is between branches,
A glimpse over the cooking-pot while Cain and Abel
Quarrel over a skin.
It has been very interesting to meet you.
Somewhere between us is the second Adam.

On My Fifty-first Birthday

I

Hare in the head-lights dance on your hind legs
Like a poor cat straggling at a rope's end.
Everything is cruelty for innocence.
If you could mark this escape from death
In your thin mind you would have eaten what I have
And, running from form to form, you would consider
The immeasurable benignity of the destructive God.

II

A great sunlit field full of lambs.
The distant perspectives are of the patched earth
With hedges creeping about. If I were to die now
No need of angels to carry me to paradise.
O Lord my God, simplify my existence.

III

The whole hill-side is roofed with lark-song.
What dangerous declivities may I not descend?
It is dark green where the horses feed.
Blackthorn and gorse open before my eyes.

IV

The gulls come inland, alight on the brown land
And bring their sea-cries to this stillness.
It was waves and the surf running they heard before
And now the lark-song and the respiration of leaves.

On the Coast

Thirty years ago I stood here,
Almost naked on the windy beach:
This is the body in which passion has decayed.

This is the clear water that sidled past me,
The white cliff, I can see it for a moment
I have no other authority for drowning.

This is certainly the body I left upon the shore
I found it the other day, crisped against the sea-weed:
This is the house in which I have slumbered these
                                                many years.

And now beside the water, walking close to the foam's
                                                edge
Before the grey turf, green turf and the brown
                                                corn-lands
I am wandering happily as an unidentified image.

But the mind will be applied in far-away London,
Bent over my files, residue of my spirit
The coming and going of thousands: it is a
                                                market-place.

I had not imagined anything but a blind future
And that is still with me, still beckoning onwards
Till the voices die and I am at rest.

It does not matter at that point what you do with my
                                                bones
These hills can have them or the dustman
So long as Dorset can brood over its grey sea.

The Adventurer

When the sun was shining and the back door was open
He went indoors and successively raped seven women.
My own desires are not much different
Since I have given up the desire of understanding
And have not succeeded in ousting my other desires.
He wept and screamed in the dock. So would not I,
But my heart is armoured by intellection;
My heart has been hardened:
On that account I catch my trains with precision
And know how to look after myself, mate.

Mortalia

In the leisurely days which precede my death
There is nothing I shall not regret. Dorset my hills
You have the shapes I have missed, the smile
Of contentment that was never mine.
Nothing but tears is hidden under your soil.

Swimming the Horses

To Pippa and David

Swimming the horses at Appleby in Westmorland
—Or Cumbria as they now call it, God damn their
                                                                  eyes.
The rest of the verses *desunt*: they were meant to say
Damn all politicians and bureaucrats
Who cannot make fires with uncertain materials.
They imagine that their voices will be heard above
The ripple of rivers and the song of cuckoos—
Which they will not be, or not for long
If they continue with their inordinate charges
To feed reputatious mouths, or none at all
And think that generations of mud-eaters
Can be stamped out to serve a committee slicker
—As they can indeed, but eaten by a dust
That will soon settle over the whole of England.
Those who kick their ancestors in the teeth
Prosper for a time, but in adversity,
Which soon comes, there is a change.

The End

I shall never hear the angelic choir
Sing, as it assuredly does, I shall walk in hell
Among tinkers and tailors and other riff-raff.
Another damnation for imagining myself among those
Whose fornications came as easy as winking

And whose pilferings of other people
Were a social bounty which did not stop at themselves.
I knew early what there was to be known about me
Only lacked courage, fortitude, *élan*
And so descended into a consuming whirlpool
Round and round, here I am at the last gurgle.

Virtue

Virtue instead of failure, a fine choice,
Virtue is its own damnation. I, who see man
In his external shape, acting and bowing,
Take no account of his inner movements
Which are lies only, must admit
Myself virtuous although my heart is a sink
Where ambition swills round with lost lust
And even the last words are spoken with envy.

Sunshine and Rain

Each day is so brief, a tiny spasm
Of light between dark. It is falling now
Having shone brightly between darks.
How is it? Once the days were long
Nights were unseen, unless in a flash of terror.
But all is night now, where I move

What I taste smells of dark. To my lips I take
A mushroom falling to powder, an orange agaric
Unnatural as nature has now become
Shining there in the dark, between sunshine and rain.

Carmen Saeculare

O sun, and moonlight shining in the woods,
The best things in heaven, always to be worshipped
As long as they give us exactly what we want

Now, at this season when selected girls
And the boys who are about to venture upon them,
Though still in bud, sing what will please London,

As you bring out one day and conceal another
Shine on the arms and legs and make them brown.
May all you see be greater than we are.

The time will come to open thighs in child-birth.
Gently, supervising god, look after the mothers.
Bringing to light is the true meaning of genitals.

Could you bring up these children without laws?
The statute-book is crowded, what wonder therefore
If all that interests them is an obscure kindness?

A hundred and ten years it may easily be
Before songs and games which come as speedily
As these three days, ah, and delicious nights.

You have sung truthfully enough, O fates.
Once it was ordained that everything should be stable
And will be again, but not now, or for ever.

Rich in apples, yes, and seething with cattle,
The succulent earth is dressed in barley whiskers.
And grow plump, embryo, from the natural gifts.

The sun will shine, as long as the boys are suppliant,
That will keep sickness away; and you girls,
Listen, for the moon will hear you if you do.

If you made London, as before it Engelland,
The Jutes coming over in ships, but only to be Romans,
Part of that remnant to join this one

The ways that have led here are multifarious,
Even Brutus from Troy, our ancestors believed,
But whatever they left they found better here.

You cannot credit the wish, that the young should be
teachable
And old age quiet. Yet it is these wishes
Spring from the earth at last, when the country flowers.

Might you not even remember the old worship?
I could name ancestors, it is not done any more.
It remains true that, before you are king, you must win.

We have been through it all, victory on land and sea,
These things were necessary for your assurance.
The King of France. Once there was even India.

Can you remember the expression 'Honour'?
There was, at one time, even Modesty.
Nothing is so dead it does not come back.

There is God. There are no Muses without him.
He it is who raises the drug-laden limbs
Which were too heavy until he stood at Saint Martin's.

It is he who holds London from Wapping to
                                        Richmond,
May he hold it a little longer, Saint George's flag
Flap strenuously in the wind from the west country.

Have you heard the phrase: 'the only ruler of princes'?
Along the Thames, in the Tower, there is the crown.
I only wish God may hear my children's prayers.

He bends now over Trafalgar Square.
If there should be a whisper he would hear it.
Are not these drifting figures the chorus?

Notes

ELLICK FARM

Revisiting a place of his childhood, the middle-aged man has no sense of having gained in knowledge with the years; nor of having achieved satisfactory full expression ('half dumb/ After half a lifetime'). But the last couplet implies that to be a writer was a destiny, which even the small boy might have accepted. The metaphor of 'turning verses' (as on a lathe), though conventional, is carefully chosen: poetry is a toil, rather than a gush of inspiration. The neat half-rhyming couplets exemplify craftsmanship, not least in the surreal emotional cry of the fifth couplet, contained by the end-stopped couplet form and by the almost disapproving brackets.

A AND B

Read this attractive but hard poem several times before considering the notes below.

Both voices (aspects of a single mind?) reckon to be philosophers: to be students of the possible meanings of human life. A senses immanence, a life-urge under supernatural and essentially benevolent direction. B tries to deflate all this with the voice of the common man. B's last attack on A is interesting: A's feelings of 'sacrifice', 'harmony' and 'a spirit' are seen as conditioned by patriotism and folly, not by a consistent philosophy. 'inconsiderate' here may partly imply *not considering* (thinking deeply) enough; but its main meaning seems to be *tiresome, awkward*—in other words, sentimental woolly ideas like A's get in B's way. His adjective 'inconsiderate' may tell us a good deal about B.

Sisson's plain style has many such precisions and delicacies. Study the words 'candour' (A's second speech), 'enacted' and 'propounded' (A's third speech). That the old man, later in the poem, should be seized by a spirit 'under the old church' seems a clear enough symbol, and a 'groin' is a ditch or valley, of course; but the 'mound above the groin' is also the focal point of a sexual landscape. The religion of this 'old church' may be very old indeed, and that of the Cerne Giant (a phallic figure on a Dorset hillside) as well as of Christ.

Finally, in the subtlety of 'Trace' (three lines from the end) we find the quiet implication that the 'way' may be already there, as a destiny, even though not understood.

A LETTER TO JOHN DONNE

Sevenoaks is a highly prosperous commuter-town in Kent.

Donne ended his life as Dean of St Paul's Cathedral and an immensely famous and popular preacher. Earlier he had written what are probably the most magnificent English poems of achieved physical love, and others of a more nervy and restless sexuality. Donne's notorious fascination with death took the bizarre form in late years of having himself painted wrapped in his shroud.

The last line of stanza 2 means 'Gives pleasure as an unhealthy sexuality can give pleasure to a heart of stone'.

The metaphor in the last two lines of stanza 3 is that of a lawsuit, a legal argument (here, to prove Donne's relevance to modern man): the evidence that he was clever (as modern Sevenoaks commuters are clever) is 'dismissed' as unimportant. ('Ability is not even the game of a fool'). *Bring out* means call as witnesses. The legal metaphor would have appealed to Donne, who had such a training and used pseudo-logical rhetoric in his own poetry.

Lust, in stanza 4, is seen as the attribute of man who has moral sense and thus feels sin (the stag, on the other hand, continues to live in paradise). A lustful man such as Donne needs God's love most and finds it most quickly.

The unity of 'body and soul' is a crucial theme in Donne; and deer to this day frequent Knole Park. Sisson feels that the new rector of St Nicholas makes the false claim ('pretension') that reverence for God has removed him from physical harm and temptation. If this were possible it would, in the poet's view, make him inhuman, 'An evaporated man', or indeed an 'animal' as in the amoral stag. Sisson's own faith is that Christ's redemption is of mankind as sinners (or 'fools') and is certainly extended to 'the highly sexed', as well as to Sevenoaks commuters (or, no doubt, Sevenoaks rectors). In the final image, Christ's redemption of man has the severity, grandeur, and concentration on each individual at a time, which are shown by a creature of prey. The paradoxical force and the conciseness of this image might have delighted Donne.

CATULLUS

lubricity (line 8): literally, wet slipperiness; metaphorically, wantonness.

pathic (line 10): homosexual favourite. Caesar, not Catullus, is meant. Catullus would have known about the scandal because he worked for the praetor of Bithynia for a year.

Catullus is said to have lived to be only thirty; and the idea that he died 'burnt out by lechery' is supported by the fierce sexual energy of his 116 poems—poems which for Sisson, as for most classical scholars, make up one of the greatest of all artistic achievements. The idea of this poem is clear enough— that Catullus represents an ultimate extension of pre-Christian energy and longing—the dream of 'An impossible love pincered from a human form.' Sisson is, of course, not exactly saying that Catullus was wrong or mistaken, and he addresses him as 'my friend'. The LETTER TO JOHN DONNE is clearly relevant here: man's lust needs and receives Christ's forgiveness, but devout men need also to know their 'genitals' and not be 'evaporated'.

ADAM

Sisson is interested in reaching back; as one critic puts it, 'clearing passages to the vital common past'. (His COLLECTED POEMS are arranged in reverse chronological order; so is his novel CHRISTOPHER HOMM.) Myth, legend, and the Bible, as well as classical literature, figure a good deal in his poems.

34

To believe that God created one takes one only a little way; after that one's direction is uncertain. The speaker doesn't think much of his potential—he is an 'artifact' of human society even though created by God, and no true shape or purpose seems to command him. He will walk in the park with the deer, avoiding greater commitment. It is consoling to him to think that in this he resembles the first man ever created.

But Adam was not 'avoiding' in the same conscious way. His 'evasions' were the result of bewilderment: they were innocent, whereas the modern man may well feel guilty in evasion. Since Adam left Paradise 'nothing has been clear': it is glimpsed only through distracting barriers and un-promising hostilities.

'The proof of a poem, any poem,' says Sisson, 'is in its rhythm.' Looking at the rhythm of this poem may help you to pin down its achievement: free verse that feels firm, flat speech with the dignity of humility. The more grand and lyrical voice, ironically, is that of the civil servant walking in the park; Adam's puzzlement comes through in his con-ventional polite farewell, as well as in the prosaic, 'When God called there was some confusion.'

ON MY FIFTY-FIRST BIRTHDAY
Presented as a single poem, this may well seem rather a group of four very short pieces, linked by the poet's recognition of his birthday and the passing of time.

'Eaten' in line 5 is puzzling. Clearly it marks humanity—eaten of the tree of knowledge?

A *form* is a hare's resting-place or retreat in long grass. Sisson may also be conscious of the word's significance for him as man and poet.

THE ADVENTURER
Compare THE END (page 27) and VIRTUE (page 28).

MORTALIA

The title literally means 'mortal things'. Sisson is probably remembering a famous line of Virgil (*sunt lacrimae rerum et mentem mortalia tangunt*), where Aeneas, shipwrecked on the North African coast, deduces from the decorations in a temple that the natives are sympathetic and understanding people: 'here tears are shed for things, and mortal things [human sufferings?] touch the heart.'

SWIMMING THE HORSES

Cumbria: The county of Westmorland, along with several other English counties built on centuries of tradition, disappeared officially in the local government reorganization of 1974.

desunt: are missing. The term is that of a classical scholar dealing with a fragmentary poem—the first line (or possibly first two lines) is all that remains of the poem.

reputatious: concerned with reputation rather than true value.

VIRTUE

Man tends to regard his own 'inner movements' (of ambition, lust, envy, etc.' as 'lies only'. He concentrates on external social performances. By such external standards the poet is 'virtuous'; but he regards this as almost a failure of nerve rather than a true goodness. (Compare THE ADVENTURER, page 26.)

SUNSHINE AND RAIN

agaric: fungus.

CARMEN SAECULARE

A version of the Centennial Hymn written by Horace to be sung by children at the supposed hundred years' anniversary festival of the city of Rome. Sisson follows the line of Horace's ideas and images, translating them where appropriate into modern English equivalents, but he deliberately alters the

36

flavour of the poem, making the sexual references more explicit, and—much more important—presenting really an ironic counterweight to Horace's genuine celebration. Sisson prays for the future of Britain and London, but with little confidence, where the Latin poem has almost the feeling of 'Land of Hope and Glory'. It is as if the two poets are standing on the same pedestal but looking in opposite directions.

The result is perhaps the most beautifully rhythmical and poignant of all Sisson's ironic poems: a personal and original piece, too, not diminished in any way by being based on a classical model. (Some English eighteenth-century poets achieved similar creative success in 'translations'.)

Andrew Waterman

Andrew Waterman was born in London in 1940. After 'a bedsitter life with a variety of jobs' he went late to university. He has lectured on English literature at the New University of Ulster in County Derry since 1968, at about which period he began seriously to write poetry; but he spends much of his time back in his native England. He has published three books of poetry.

Waterman is a discursive, fairly colloquial poet; his rangy, free-moving poems contrast with most others in this book. He tends to write personally and anecdotally, and his poems are easy to grasp, at least provided you follow the movement of the sentence carefully. Though his life so far has been, in his own words, 'rather intensely individualistic' and 'maverick', he may yet seem to represent for us a characteristic late twentieth-century English consciousness, with which we may well feel a good deal in common: friendly, ironic, informal; a bit rootless; free of most illusions; sensitive but ideologically uncommitted. The open, apparently relaxed forms he uses suit this consciousness; but they are forms under a measure of control. Most are written in regular line-groups, mostly with five-stress lines—there is no rhyme and the lines feel free of metrical formality, but the poet preserves a sense of shape and pattern. His language, even when very colloquial, is not slack: it is clear and frequently vivid. And in their telling imagery and their emotion the poems are carefully poised, in apprehension, intelligent uncertainty, or complexity of feeling.

Man Cycling Home in Donegal

A black coat flapping on a rusted bicycle
steadily pedalled beneath a vast sky,

he does not look over the spiky hedges,
intent on the day's end at the tarmac's end.

Intention contracts him out of the landscape,
a speck of absence; yet nags to alignment

all its passing through ignores,
the wilderness massing its greens and blues

under wide light ebbing where distant
peaks are null with snow. The contours

of centuries gathered behind pour through
this man, defining his substance, waste spaces.

His life is heavy with generations
of mist, of marriages silted with hailstones.

His slow deliberateness conforms
to outlines of ridge and glen, their scope

and lack of detail. He has no ideas,
being certain only of the earth and the stars

and—though tonight light flies from his hammer
about the cottage—snow dulling his pulses.

Mother

I should be grateful. You
adopted me in a hard time,
the sound of guns from Dunkirk shaking
London, the bombs. You have told
how once you lay over my pram as a German
aeroplane swooped to machine-gun the street.
What made you, you never did say.

It was only 'You should be grateful' became
the theme you played on a subtle keyboard
(you'd not been an actress in vain):
grateful for supper, for half-days in Brighton,
for wellington boots in rainy weather,
'For all I have done for you.'
There was also your tone saying 'Don't.'

And when father left you said nothing,
except—remember?—when
I finally asked, that day in the park
at the rusted green cafeteria seats,
to distract me, 'Look at those sparrows,'
and did not notice rage boiling the dregs
of a nine-year-old's childhood away.

So I locked you from me in turn, as I locked
my schoolwork away in a case.
Where was I going? 'Out.'
And when leaving for good I came
to tell you, you carried on hanging up washing,
not taking the peg from your mouth just said
'Remember to leave your doorkey.'

At seventy now, arthritis
has withered the touch and range
from your piano-player's hands,
your first teeth are gone (years after mine).
Hoarding a fossil faith
in Stalin, the god that failed,
you keep up the garden, read Dickens, see plays,

and we can be easier together,
and I am truly grateful.
If what you pinched and scraped once seemed
me, I know now it was for me,
understand things you still cannot say
as your talkative letters come, each signed
not 'with love,' just 'as ever'.

A Butterfly

Even under the shed there's something outdoors
about the work. One side stands open

to stars and wind. You pause on your barrow to watch
dawn come up, or a shower across the city.

You're never bricked in. On slack shifts in summer
men wander off along overgrown sidings, embankments,

for a sun and a glance through the *Mirror*: a couple
have planted a vegetable-garden back of
                          Humberstone Coal Wharf.

Grass invades. Dustiest corners are settled
with unauthorised flowers. The Grain Shed sparrows

strut plundering leaking sacks, great rats
buck-jump away from right under your feet.

On a fine day wagons trundle in hung with glittering
waterdrops: somewhere rain is falling.

Even one bleak night, surrounded
by foggy blackness, and cartons, crates,

rolls of netting stacked up on the shed-platform,
hard graft, something broke in when old Gumble
                                                            found

in the straw that wadded a cased-up carboy of acid
a sleepy butterfly. It crawled

on to his palm. 'Beautiful little bugger,
in't it?' It fluttered in his sour beer breath.

'Look at this, Jacko. Red Admiral.' Wherever
he carried it, cupped precious in his hands,

men stopped, gathering under wan lights:
blue overalls, stubbled faces focused on

a butterfly, straw strewn upon the concrete,
and birds starting racketing for the new day in the
                                                            girders.

Gardens

'This is your garden. Dig it.'
Eight hummocky feet by three in a rancid corner.
Bored, I poked about, chopped at worms, bought seeds

at Woolworth's in vividly illustrated packets.
Such as came up looked shoddier, or were just weeds.
And besides, I preferred running off down the forest.

Since then I've had no gardens, 'And no regrets,'
I usually say, 'they enslave you.'
All those bank-clerks pruning their privet each Sunday!

Not but what peering in on some shimmering lawn
with water-sprinklers rotating for ever, splodged
with immaculate flowerbeds, there's not envy—

though the silver-haired bloke at the roller framed
                                                against
open french windows is not my style,
nor such casual-seeming perfectedness, not to mention

rustic bird-baths, phoney tudor lanterns.
Still, as I move on, does the wrought-iron of his gate
bar his world or mine? I wonder.

And I quite like to haunt public gardens;
or those of stately homes, with statuary,
ornamental cascades and grottoes, hedges cut

into classically soluble mazes,
or some landscaped romantic vista along a lake,
trees shovelled up into the clouds.

And back looking out of whatever rooms I've got
at some rubbly yard with bins, or untended jungle
where you hear the tumbledown walls' stones grinding
in frost,
I hanker after illusive gardens,
from Adam and Eve to *Alice*; and that one
in the story everyone's read, through a magical gate

in a wall in a drab city street.
Some fertile green congruence: I can almost feel
its moss, catch scents in the breeze, hear the sound of
water.

'Concrete the bloody things over and leave yourself
free.'

Yet now, if I found myself settling for one,
I'd set about digging.

Coming Down

Our cylinder of hushed steel tilts, slides down;
and lives contracted to the beating of the engines

see startling, iridescent laciness
spread on the waters of the night, lit London:

whorls and radials of orange, blue,
turquoise, an insubstantial rainbow-froth

that might swirl away down its black holes.
Yet flashes stammering there the motivation

of an electric train, and smaller lights
moving, speak of human purposes.

Unreal; till grounded and bussed in, and stood
jostled on hard pavement, a quarrel breaks

behind me: 'I will.' 'You won't.' 'You'll see I will.'
Giving back local scale and weight.

I check my map. Above me, bowed lamps roof
intricacies shutting out the dark waste spaces.

Summer Truce

The weather holds. From Strangford Lough to Swilly
soft arms of coast cradle still water.
Sunning before our shore's-edge cottage we
'enjoy it while it lasts', watch floated fronds
of seaweed among the rocks slightly
lifting with a glitter like broken glass.

And the radio talks into blue day—
to campions, sea-pinks, primroses run wild
over springy turf—of another sectarian killing,
a club blown up, several injured.
The tiny insistent voice is a black mote
in the mind, troubling the horizon

within which our concerns are local as
the cliff-path hesitating its few miles
to Portrush. We have our jokes, lovemaking,
morning-squabbles; John and Mary are at
each other's throats in phone-kiosks, kitchens;
another friend founders in private madness;

and 'Fuck off to Limavady' as the man said
last night to his girl, means over the edge
of the little world. But later ourselves beyond
Limavady, we find in Derry
the truce keeps up, with festive bunting and
the soldiers relaxed and eating ice-cream.

We drink campari in sweet evening air
where mountains pour down to the lough-side;
seething at Reggie you shred a pound note with your
                                              teeth.
—And this morning sit writing it up in your journal
here on the city wall, where ten days back
that policeman was shot from no personal anger.

All peace is imperfect. At last Belfast: the pub
where we talk poetry is pocked from old bombings—
nothing's worth fixing these days. In the gents'
a washbasin grimed and fractured, filled with glass,
taps issuing only a parched gush of air.
Outside, still sunshine. Everyone waits for the break.

1975

48

From the Other Country

But you do not consider how long I have lived in this
                                      country.
Its skies move through my skull, and the changing
                                              light
over the water; like whales the humped mountains
surface in my dreams, and never were trees
thwart like these in flight from the salt harsh gales.

The customs of the people, it is true,
are not mine; in farms and one-street towns
they enact strict rituals of thrift, worship, pleasure.
Lights burn late where slow accounts are reckoned,
the drunk crashes prone in dying embers,

and beneath tribal tokens, ancient recitations.
Often indeed through main street and glen
drums throb savage annunciation, the door
opens to a rain of bullets, car-lights pick out
the corpse in a ditch. 'It's a madness going on,'

they say. Did you think madness so dull?
Look: how finite among the weltering green
these settlements, no margins to nourish the odd.
Knowing their place, they grow, pray, wed, kill, die.
Even their knowing smiles have a terrible innocence

which you do not understand. Nor, though you hear,
how their soft gutturals and singing intonation
infect my accent. I am welcomed
in bars and corner-shops, with 'It's a soft night.'
And yes, I have loved their girls.

See, where fine w hite clouds drift high above the
                                          meadow
the small farm daydreams all doors open:
they are all gone round the bend of the field, out of
                                          change.
Behind the clock on the mantel dust thickens on letters
strangely-deciphered, from children 'across the water'.

From where, too, on my screen come shimmering
images of the old labyrinthine cities,
sanities. Which I can revisit, resume
undetected; noticing how they find
bestial or glamorous our banalities,

and do not see the detail beneath stark outlines.
I am no longer sure that I wish to return,
even though it is winter here now, the sky and land
seeping greyly together. Unsettled, defined
by difference, I find I can live with this,

am strangely involved in, call it, a climate.
Yes, as the mad wind rises, sets the sea
resonating, whips waves white, and plucks
tiles from thin roofs, above which gulls
weave lamentation's dissonant vocables.

In Highgate Wood

A flicker of sun through leaves in Highgate Wood,
this moment of recognition: I who know
no kin find myself open intently
in a willed, almost religious relinquishing,

as if to diffuse among this ceaseless play
some latent thing so near in me it asks
to be named all that I now forego
as what it might have been: I say, 'My son.'

Whispering translucencies take up the merely
personal into their green going-on
ageing within each season's restlessness.
Another spring. I lean against

a hornbeam's fluted trunk to follow up
the frail slant of a silver birch bole hung
with tatters of bark like peeling paint.
Slow bramble smothers cut lengths of felled tree,

and the bones of a dumped pram are patiently
digested. Always the forest, underfoot
its dead green softening to renew; and nothing
I can bestow: this is, as from a child,

a receiving. See how delicately wrought
that cherry-tree declares its blossoming,
drifts of flowers like conjurings from snow
almost, so pure and candid:

luminous thing, it tricks the eye
to seem itself condensation of mere air
floating it, yet is earthed in darkness.
Brief one of many, time unique as flesh.

Playing Through Old Games of Chess

A crane-fly trembles in the windowpane
as it has since before there were windows . . . .
I play through old games of chess: their rich diapason
a blossoming in the room, as of huge heavy-headed
                                                  roses.

Outside, the hottest summer since records began,
and the traffic-lights signalling insane morse,
a jabber of red green amber, somewhere a computer
has overheated, fouling the traffic and tempers

are overheated, and all along the Thames
the bridges shove themselves over from metal expansion.
Ah, the ecologists say, it is carbon dioxide
irreversibly building up in the upper atmosphere

due to industrial waste, and all kinds of waste
accumulate irreversibly, and we record it,
even the mineral ores of language processed through
to a standing slag beyond recycling;

and economists say it is the economy overheated.
The plane trees shimmer through rising petrol fumes,
and children's voices ascend to tinkle against the bowl
of a blue sky hazed with entropy, our last heat-death.

I reset the pieces and start again:
Steinitz versus Tchigorin, Ruy Lopez, Morphy
                                        Defence,
Havana, 1892, and decorously
the opposite knights step forth, the kings are castled
                                        to safety

for a while. And still for a while
beyond the cities in meadows (but a hum of traffic
                                        hanging)
the cows, as then, stand four-square over their
                                        shadows,
while one by one white petals slip into sun-dappled
                                        water

to float, for a while; and the woods are dark with
                                        summer,
greenness sloping to greenness to a far
horizon marked with the faint stroke of a steeple
as it has been since before there were

—steeples, I almost said. At least as when
all history seemed a sort of sunlit incline upwards,
with problems like the Balkans, abolishing cholera,
                                        crime,
certainly soluble, and change meant improvement,

hygiene, gas cooking, fast travel, the bioscope.
Beneath 'Truman, Hanbury, Buxton & Comps. Entire'
the old photograph shows clay pipes and boaters
                                        around an ale-bench,
and Spoonbeam is not out at lunch for Lancs for ever,

while at dusk, his cycle-lamp catching gold motes
along deep lanes where roots twist and convolvulus
                                                    clings,
comes Cholmondeley to talk, over whiskey by leaded
                                                  windows,
of *The Origin of Species* or *The Idylls of the King*.

The pawn-structure looks sound, across the board
                                        andante
the full orchestration unfolds, with recurring motifs
                                      and grace-notes,
rounding Good Hope the *Ariel* bringing home tea
                                        from China,
cablegrams under the sea, while in Afghan hill-posts

or where a delta's archipelagos of bamboo huts
coalesce to a port of old palaces, crumbling pagodas,
men with iron moustaches bat out their time
outstaring all sundowns from the verandah.

Of course, through the looking-glass all was different,
and moving forward got you nowhere, the miners
stonily piling their barrows after the latest eviction
cannot see their great-grandsons' Cortinas,
                                  package-tour fritterings,

and the husband who tendered with flowers the most
                                  honourable intentions
is hanging his stovepipe hat on the bedposts of whores;
and every life dark-edged, the hushed death-rooms, the
                                        infant graves;
and perhaps it is all the tinman's dream

who stationed at the street corner pedals his grinding-
                                        wheel
for ever. And as for the countless hordes
of Indians and Chinese, it is not their game
at all, they have nothing to learn but patience.

Exchange of queens: the general liquidation
which follows seems to favour white, a sacrificial
manoeuvre clinches things, for the while. If today
in Flanders the farmer again wades through barley
                                  where all nature

was murdered, still the old dynasts have toppled like
                                    chess-kings,
and however we go through the motions again
(the squares are being done up, houses wormy with
                                    their past
are scoured, the cellars blocked off as if there were
                                  bones down in them,

layers of cheap flowered paper torn from each wall),
or trace the lines not followed, unrealised combinations
in notes as much as the moves played part of the game,
the quality of that long, lost summer cannot be restored

—when June rang like a gong for Pax Britannica,
and Europe's chordage held the world enthralled;
and in London, St Petersburg, Vienna or Baden Baden
the old chess-masters' arias thrilled. Until Lasker, who

would research Relativity, talk with Einstein, flee
the Nazis, shifted a piece irrevocably changing
the chemistry of the game, its lovely architectonics;
while a crane-fly trembled in the windowpane.

Notes

MAN CYCLING HOME IN DONEGAL

The crux is in lines 5–7. Because the man does not look over the hedges, and is thinking only of his cottage at the end of the road, he seems 'contracted out' (i.e. by a voluntary withdrawal) from the landscape; in the other sense of 'contracted' he becomes only a 'speck', and it is a speck of 'absence' (compare the phrase 'absent-minded'). For a moment the feeling seems to be that the man's life is trivial, insubstantial. But on the word 'yet' the poem turns, in an unexpected direction: in spite of his indifference to it, the man's 'intention' makes significant the landscape around him, 'nags' it into 'alignment'. He is defined by the hills and valleys, which are a link with previous generations; and the slow pace of his life is created by that environment and heritage.

Put like this, it sounds reassuring; but is that how the poem feels to you?

A BUTTERFLY

One of a sequence of eleven 'Railway Poems', 'the fruit of four summers' work in a Leicester goodsyard'. A poem of happiness, without a trace of fantasy or (I reckon—what do you think?) sentimentality. 'You're never bricked in.' Few places, you might think, are more polluted, denatured, than a railway goodsyard: but if there are no trees the birds will 'racket' in the girders, the vegetables and flowers and grass and sparrows and rats—and the sleepy butterfly—seem to manage to thrive; and in the sour beer breath and habitual obscenity of old Gumble there is room for the word 'beautiful' and the recognition of what is 'precious'. There is room in the poet's perception, also, to recognize the incidental magic of wet wagons on a sunny day. It is an exceptionally fine poem, I think, because it is so vivid without being (with

56

the possible exception of 'racketing' in the last line) at all forced: existence described delicately and faithfully becomes naturally exhilarating.

GARDENS
illusive: deceptive (with echoes of 'illusory' and 'elusive').
congruence: things fitting together, harmony.

COMING DOWN
'swirl away down its black holes' is a forked or punning metaphor, with an extreme contrast between its two associations—the domestic friendly gurgle of bath-water, and the baffling, alarming 'black holes' of outer space in which matter is swallowed. The poem is *about* this sort of overlap and contrast. After the disorienting beauty of London's lights seen at night from the air, the quarrel in the airport terminal restores the scale of individual human lives. The poet checks his map both literally and metaphorically, registering where he is in the comprehensible local maze of Greater London, shutting out the incomprehensible 'dark waste spaces'.

Re-read MAN CYCLING HOME IN DONEGAL as a comparison.

SUMMER TRUCE
sectarian: between members of religious groups (sects)—the phrase is now standard in news reports of Northern Ireland troubles.
Derry: here, the big city of Londonderry, where troubles might be expected more than at the quiet coast.

The 'truce' (a real military truce during the hot summer of 1975) is presented throughout the poem as a series of images of violence suspended in stanzas of apparent calm: the 'glitter like broken glass', the bad news on the radio, John and Mary 'at each other's throats', the friend 'in private madness', the crude aggression of 'Fuck off to Limavady', and the pound note shredded with the teeth. It is a poem of suspended sunlit unease.

The 'other country' is, of course, Northern Ireland; yet there the speaker is himself defined as 'from the other country' (England).

Stanza 1. *thwart*: bent across.

Stanza 3. *annunciation*: announcement. After 'tribal tokens' and 'ancient recitations', there is a hint—bitterly inappropriate—of the Angel Gabriel's Annunciation to the Virgin Mary that she would be the mother of the son of God.

Stanza 7. From England come televised programmes showing the 'labyrinthine cities' of England, which are 'sanities' by comparison with the 'madness' of Ulster (stanzas 3, 4 and 7).

The poet, whose early life we have seen in MOTHER and perhaps in GARDENS to have been 'unsettled', feels 'defined' by the disturbed 'climate' of Northern Ireland. Compare the man in Donegal 'defined' by his environment.

IN HIGHGATE WOOD

Highgate Wood is in north London; ancient woodland surrounded by housing.

The compressed syntax needs following carefully—be sure you understand the first sentence (i.e. the first two stanzas). 'Relinquishing' usually means giving up with some reluctance; here the sense is of a rare, undefined delight, but the faint hint of reluctance conveys how unnerving and 'almost religious' it is to feel so 'open'.

If the poet had a son he could 'diffuse' his 'recognition' by watching him play and 'receiving' the child's happiness and fulfilment. As it is, the poem is what he can 'bestow': the poem turns out to be the 'latent thing so near in me'.

'Recognition' of what? Stanza 3, and the last line of all, help with the answer.

PLAYING THROUGH OLD GAMES OF CHESS

Chess-enthusiasts frequently when alone play through, moving all the pieces themselves, old games of chess which are recorded in books, in order to study and relish them.

Stanza 1. *crane-fly*: daddy long-legs.

diapason: rich complex music.

Stanza 5. *entropy*: the gradual exhaustion of the energy of the world.

Stanzas 9–13. A selective resumé of elements of the world of 1892. The fact that it is selective and therefore inaccurate is emphasized in stanzas 14–16.

Stanza 12. *andante*: steadily. *Motifs and grace-notes* continue the musical metaphor (begun in stanza 1 with *diapason*).

Stanza 17. In the chess-game the queens are exchanged (i.e. each taken by the opponent)—a drastic sacrifice on both sides (which leads us to the First World War—Flanders was one of the main battlefields).

Stanzas 18–21. The Flanders fields are farmland again, the Victorian houses are being done-up, the chess-game of 1892 can be replayed: imagination can even dwell on the possible alternative moves which might have been made—this is part of the point of studying old games of chess and part of the poignancy of studying the past. But fundamentally life has changed. The 'old dynasts'—the old European empires, political and commercial—have gone; and Emanuel Lasker, who dominated world chess from 1894 (soon after the game the poet is playing through) till 1921 (well after the First World War), was also associated with Einstein's crucial research into Relativity, which changed the thought of the early twentieth century almost as much as Darwin's *Origin of Species* (see stanza 11) had changed the thought of people in 1892. (*The Idylls of the King*, incidentally, are poems by Tennyson, very popular in 1892.) And Lasker lived to have to flee the Nazis. 'The game' has changed. The crane-flies, on the other hand, are much the same.

Stanza 20. Pax Romana was the international peace and free trade between all the countries in the Roman Empire. The British Empire was at its height in 1892: hence *Pax Britannica*.

chordage: presumably, musical harmony (chords), but there seems also to be a pun on 'cordage'—as if Europe were held together only by force and tension.

Craig Raine

Craig Raine was born in 1944 in County Durham, and studied English at Oxford, where he is now a lecturer. He has published two books of poetry. His work is original and attractive in a time when sober, though sensitive, orthodoxy is widespread in new poetry. The correspondences—the echoes, resemblances, chimings—which symbolist poets of the nineteenth century found in apparently very different realities; the subversive dislocations of conventional ways of seeing which were practised by surrealist painters in the twentieth century—these are the grand ancestors of Raine's more modest, less pretentious, observations. His poems are often very funny; but they are a real look at the world, not a comic script, and the line, from AN ENQUIRY INTO TWO INCHES OF IVORY, 'if only we believed our eyes' could stand as an epigraph. And, of course, irony and comedy often make a means of expression of an otherwise intolerable awareness—of the gap between potential and reality, or of the inevitability of death. Beneath Raine's wit and acuteness lies gentleness: he is a most humane writer.

An Enquiry into Two Inches of Ivory

We live in the great indoors:
the vacuum cleaner grazes
over the carpet, lowing,
its udder a swollen wobble . . .

At night, the switches stare
from every wall like flat-faced
barn-owls, and light ripens
the electric pear.

Esse is percipi—Berkeley knew
the gentle irony of objects, how
they told amusing lies and drew laughter,
if only we believed our eyes.

Daily things. Objects
in the museum of ordinary art.
Two armless Lilliputian queens
preside, watching a giant bathe.
He catches the slippery cubist fish
with perfumed eggs. Another
is a yogi on the scrubbing brush.
Water painlessly breaks his bent
Picasso legs.

Clothes queue up in the wardrobe,
an echo to the eye, or a jangle of Euclid.
The wall-phone wears a pince-nez
even in the dark—the flex
is Jewish orthodox.

Day begins.
The milkman delivers
penguins with their chinking atonal fuss.
Cups commemorate the War
of Jenkins' Ear,
Without thinking, the giant
puts a kettle on the octopus.

Flying to Belfast, 1977

It was possible to laugh
as the engines whistled to the boil,

and wonder what the clouds looked like—
shovelled snow, Apple Charlotte,

Tufty Tails . . . I enjoyed
the Irish Sea, the ships were faults

in a dark expanse of linen.
And then Belfast below, a radio

with its back ripped off,
among the agricultural abstract

of the fields. Intricate,
neat and orderly. The windows

gleamed like drops of solder—
everything was wired up.

I thought of wedding presents,
white tea things

grouped on a dresser,
as we entered the cloud

and were nowhere—
a bride in a veil, laughing

at the sense of event, only
half afraid of an empty house

with its curtains boiling
from the bedroom window.

The Onion, Memory

Divorced, but friends again at last,
we walk old ground together
in bright blue uncomplicated weather.
We laugh and pause
to hack to bits these tiny dinosaurs,
prehistoric, crenellated, cast
between the tractor ruts in mud.

On the green, a junior Douglas Fairbanks,
swinging on the chestnut's unlit chandelier,
defies the corporation spears—
a single rank around the bole,
rusty with blood.
Green, tacky phalluses curve up, romance.
A gust—the old flag blazes on its pole.

In the village bakery
the pasty babies pass
from milky slump to crusty cadaver,
from crib to coffin—without palaver.
All's over in a flash,
too silently . . .

Tonight the arum lilies fold
back napkins monogrammed in gold,
crisp and laundered fresh.
Those crustaceous gladioli, on the sly,
reveal the crimson flower-flesh
inside their emerald armour plate.
The uncooked herrings blink a tearful eye.
The candles palpitate.
The Oistrakhs bow and scrape
in evening dress, on Emi-tape.

Outside the trees are bending over backwards
to please the wind: the shining sword
grass flattens on its belly.
The white-thorn's frillies offer no resistance.
In the fridge, a heart-shaped jelly
strives to keep a sense of balance.

I slice up the onions. You sew up a dress.
This is the quiet echo—flesh—
white muscle on white muscle,
intimately folded skin,
finished with a satin rustle.
One button only to undo, sewn up with shabby thread.
It is the onion, memory,
that makes me cry.

Because there's everything and nothing to be said,
the clock with hands held up before its face,
stammers softly on, trying to complete a phrase—
while we, together and apart,
repeat unfinished gestures got by heart.

And afterwards, I blunder with the washing on the
                                                    line—
headless torsos, faceless lovers, friends of mine.

The Behaviour of Dogs

Their feet are four-leafed clovers
that leave a jigsaw in the dust.

They grin like Yale keys and tease
us with joke-shop Niagara tongues.

A whippet jack-knifes across the grass
to where the afghan's palomino fringe

is part Opera House curtain, part
Wild Bill Hicock. Its head

precedes the rest, balanced like
a tray, aloft and to the left.

The labrador cranks a village pump,
the boxer shimmies her rump,

docked to a door knocker, and
the alsatian rattles a sabre—

only the ones with crewcuts fight.
Sportif, they scratch their itches

like one-legged cyclists sprinting
for home, pee like hurdlers,

shit like weightlifters, and relax
by giving each other piggy backs . . .

Birth

In Tommy Morton's byre—
but the child, when it came, was perfect.

Milking the Friesian,
squeezing the softness, pinging the pail—

soft chandelier of stalactites:
the shifting legs prop up the hundredweights of dark.

And the waters broke in a little beck:
it helter-skelters slowly,

round and down my only pair of tights,
gets inside my overshoes.

The wet stone flags and the hiss of the Tilley
breathing in, and always breathing in.

68

The swallows came and went like carpenters,
their beaks full of twigs. A trickling tap.

But the child, when it came, was perfect.
The funny fossil of the anus,

cloacal curl coiled up in bloodied alabaster,
and the after-birth dyeing the milk in the pail.

Centuries later the light brought two of the shepherds,
the tall one picking his nose, and Douthwaite smirking.

They ran for a doctor, fetched Joe from the pub,
smelling of drink and brilliantine,

his old straw hat on the back of his head,
the nimbus of its fraying rim.

And Dr Anderson and Dr Smythe
and Dr Middleton, the senior partner,

all three of them came from the pub,
with penicillin, needles, gut.

Square Dance at Cana

He takes the great folio Bible,
the one with studded boards and uncut pages,

undoes the clasp and rests it on his knees—
a black accordion to celebrate the Sabbath.

On the windowsill, a Waterford vase,
filled from the tap in the yard outside,

takes to itself the sunset's sweet sauterne,
and bishops move on a tipsy tangent,

a knight totters forward and then to the left
knocking over a Queen—and all things marry.

Epileptic Fit

A notice in the Wayside Pulpit
announces blankness to the bleaching sun,

blankness and three rusty drawing pins.
The graveyard's empty picture house

is packed with rows of shiny seats,
threadbare granite ruined with initials

and patchily plush with moss . . .
He lies, relaxed as coppernob Van Johnson

when he took the part of Rip van Winkle—
his jersey tucked into his underpants,

his features busy as the flywheel of a watch,
one eyebrow jigging like a rabbit's nose.

It is the waking which is terrible:
the stretching arms, the screaming yawn,

the way his spine curves like a ladle,
the paper face that crumples up . . .

Beside the cemetery, allotments,
and a crusted sty with rooting pigs

who rummage in the swill
like women at a jumble sale.

Floppy hats, high-heeled trotters,
massive hams, a double row of buttons

done up neatly, salmon pink on beige—
they squeal and stub their noses out,

flushed and burning with the change of life . . .

The Italian Doctor with the Roman Nose

Trumpets of the Coundon Silver Band
barabb—babba—baa   barabb—babba—baa

and the doctor washing his hands,
trickling tap and Wright's Coal Tar.

Outside where Redworth Road meets St John's Place,
the drum is afraid, the drum is so afraid—

worn skin and hollow bumping carapace.
Barabb—babba—baa the bugles brayed . . .

Who will remember
that once I heard

the Requiem by Verdi
in the Free Trade Hall at Manchester,

or how I liked two sugars in my tea,
well stirred?

Who will dream my face
as white as wedding sheets, my lips

vague as laundered bloodstains?
Who will trace

in sleep the outline of my hips?
Or hear the heart in every blood-filled gland

jerking like a second-hand?
Will anything remain?

Tuba mirum spargens sonum
per sepulcra regionum

barabb—babba—baa
barabb—babba—baa . . .

A Martian Sends a Postcard Home

Caxtons are mechanical birds with many wings
and some are treasured for their markings—

they cause the eyes to melt
or the body to shriek without pain.

I have never seen one fly, but
sometimes they perch on the hand.

Mist is when the sky is tired of flight
and rests its soft machine on ground:

then the world is dim and bookish
like engravings under tissue paper.

Rain is when the earth is television.
It has the property of making colours darker.

Model T is a room with the lock inside—
a key is turned to free the world

for movement, so quick there is a film
to watch for anything missed.

But time is tied to the wrist
or kept in a box, ticking with impatience.

In homes, a haunted apparatus sleeps,
that snores when you pick it up.

If the ghost cries, they carry it
to their lips and soothe it to sleep

with sounds. And yet, they wake it up
deliberately, by tickling with a finger.

Only the young are allowed to suffer
openly. Adults go to a punishment room

with water but nothing to eat.
They lock the door and suffer the noises

alone. No one is exempt
and everyone's pain has a different smell.

At night, when all the colours die,
they hide in pairs

and read about themselves—
in colour, with their eyelids shut.

Floods

Bright as meringues, the swans sweep
sideways down the passionate water.

The boathouse punts are magnetized,
and the rain scores a bull's-eye every time.

There is a bank of froth against the bridge.
It has thrown in the sponge . . .

The flood shines like Occam's razor.
Every quibble returns to the torrent,

and even the slow digressions at our feet
are part of an overall argument.

They cover all the points of grass.
What single-minded brilliance,

what logic!
Not one of us can look away.

In the Mortuary

Like soft cheeses they bulge
sideways on the marble slabs,

helpless, waiting to be washed.
Cotton wool clings in wisps

to the orderly's tongs,
its creaking purpose done . . .

He calls the woman 'Missus',
an abacus of perspiration

on his brow, despite the cold.
And she is the usual woman—

two terra cotta nipples
like patches from a cycle kit,

puzzled knees, finely
crumpled skin around the eyes,

and her stomach like a watermark
held up to the light.

Distinguishing marks: none.
Colour of eyes: closed.

Somewhere, inside an envelope
inside a drawer, her spectacles . . .

Somewhere else, not here, someone
knows her hair is parted wrongly

and cares about these cobwebs
in the corners of her body.

Laying a Lawn

(*for Ian McEwan*)

I carry these crumbling tomes
two at a time from the stack

and lay them open on the ground.
Bound with earth to last,

they're like the wordless books
my daughter lugs about unread

or tramples underfoot. I stamp
the simple text of grass

with woodwormed brogues
while my daughter looks on,

holding her hard, muscular doll
by its only leg . . .

She hands me a caterpillar
rucked like a curtain, just as

one day she'll bring me teeth—
segments of sweet-corn

in the palm of her hand.
While she faces me, I needn't see

the thin charcoal crucifix
her legs and buttocks make,

only the hair on her body
like tiny scratches in gold,

her little cunt's neat button-hole,
and the navel's wrinkled pip . . .

For the moment, our bodies
are immortal in their ignorance—

neither one of us can read
this Domesday Book.

Notes

AN ENQUIRY INTO TWO INCHES OF IVORY

Title: Jane Austen referred to her art as 'a little bit (two inches wide) of ivory'.

esse: to be.

percipi: to be perceived.

Berkeley: eighteenth-century philosopher much concerned with the relation between perception and reality.

Lilliputian: see the first volume of Jonathan Swift's GULLIVER'S TRAVELS.

cubist . . . Picasso: see the paintings of Picasso, Braque and friends in the 1910s.

Euclid: the pioneer of traditional geometry.

Jewish orthodox: i.e. like the side-lock (ringlet of hair) of an orthodox Jew.

atonal: without a central musical key.

the War of Jenkins' Ear: Great Britain and Spain fought (1739–41) after an incident in which Robert Jenkins claimed that his ear had been cut off by Spanish coastguards. Each cup has only one 'ear'.

FLYING TO BELFAST, 1977

The 'empty house' is of course the house which the metaphorical bride will take over after the wedding; and the bedroom will be where her marriage is consummated. The 'boiling' curtains take us gently back to the image in the second line. The idea of coming to the boil, coming to an exciting crisis, underlies the whole poem.

THE ONION, MEMORY

crenellated: with serrated or horned back. (The dinosaurs here are shapes in the dried mud of a track.)

Douglas Fairbanks: a dashing chandelier-swinging film-star of the 1930s. (The chestnut—whose flowers, when they are out, are often described as candles, so 'chandelier' is doubly appropriate—has rusty iron spikes round it.)

Oistrakhs: celebrated violinists. *Bow and scrape* is usually used of obsequious servants; in a sense, the Oistrakhs have become that by being so readily available on tape. But mainly the poet is punning on *bow* (to rhyme with slow) of a violin, the use of which can look (and sometimes sound) like scraping.

Increasingly, in the apparently random fooling of the poem, the images seem appropriate to the reunion of the divorced couple—fresh-laundered lilies, palpitating candles, bowing and scraping violinists, trees bending over backwards to please, a heart trying to keep balance. . . . By the end we know that fooling can be very sad indeed.

THE BEHAVIOUR OF DOGS

palomino: horse with long blond mane and tail.

Wild Bill Hicock: Wild West hero. (Note how the verse of the next sentence enacts what it is describing.)

sportif: the French rather than the English word, perhaps because of the associations of the Tour de France in the following image!

FOUR POEMS FROM 'ANNO DOMINI'

'Anno Domini' ('in the year of Our Lord') is a sequence of ten poems, all—except the first—written in two-line groups, though usually without metre or rhyme. The sequence is described as 'the fragmented biography of a faith-healer, whose greatest miracles are imaginative'. A particular faith-healer—Christ of Nazareth—is in fact repeatedly called to mind: the prologue for example describes, in mock-medieval phonetic regional accent ('orwriggle bud addernoudle' = 'oracle but adenoidal'), a modern John the Baptist, working weekdays as a corporation gardener. The settings and characters are modern and English and, we gather, drawn from the poet's own experience (Co. Durham and Oxford, for example). The parallelisms may not always be kind or respectful to the

79

Christian tradition (one poem is called SUNBLEST BREAD AND TWO TAIL-ENDS OF COD and ends 'Who is feeding five thousand kids from a bottomless paper bag?'), but they have at times the urgency and poignancy of real religious need, as the selection here may show.

BIRTH

byre: cow-shed. The speaker is both a modern farm-girl and the Virgin Mary.

waters: the first stage of childbirth is a gush of fluid.

A *Tilley* is a paraffin lamp.

The swallows are seen as building a nest—for the child? 'like carpenters' reminds us of 'Joe's' job; but also anticipates the cross-building at the time of the Crucifixion. Finally, carpenters carry nails (as swallows twigs) in their mouths.

The *cloaca* leads to the anus.

'Centuries later' paradoxically teases us into trying to expand this modern, Tilley-lamped birth backwards in time.

Traditional Nativity paintings show gold haloes round the heads of the Holy Family—a bit like an 'old straw hat on the back of his head'. The poem reminds me a good deal, in fact, of Nativity paintings, where very frequently the painter would translate the scene into his own time and locality. The 'penicillin', 'needles' and 'gut' of the last line are, of course, the gifts of the modern Magi.

SQUARE DANCE AT CANA

square dance: traditional folk-dance, such as might be danced at a country wedding. Of course chess-pieces on a board could be seen as dancing on squares.

Cana: Christ, attending a wedding at Cana, turned water into wine to boost supplies.

Waterford vase: a fine cut-glass vase, contrasting with the humble water-supply outside.

sauterne: sweet wine, the colour of evening sunlight.

Bishops in chess move diagonally, knights ahead and then to one side.

The message on the board outside the church has disappeared
with sunlight and time. In the graveyard an epileptic, with
red hair like the film-star Van Johnson, is recovering from a
fit. As he recovers, our attention is transferred to pigs in a
neighbouring sty. Christ is said to have withdrawn evil
spirits from a crazed man and transferred them into the
bodies of swine.

The visual pun of pigs/middle-aged women at the jumble
sale is cruel but very funny. *Change of life* is the time when
middle-aged women may suffer from flushes and excitability.

THE ITALIAN DOCTOR WITH THE ROMAN NOSE
Pontius Pilate was the Roman (therefore Italian, of course)
ruler of Jerusalem who agreed to Christ's execution. Having
the power to grant an amnesty to one condemned man, he
offered the Jewish crowd a pardon either for Christ or for a
hardened criminal, Barabbas. The tradition is that the crowds
yelled 'Barabbas!' Pilate then washed his hands in public as
a claim that the responsibility for Christ's death would not
be his.

The scene is a modern industrial town with the local brass
band thumping up the street. The drum-beat merges with
the drumming of the poet's blood in the fear of death. A
carapace is a shell—here the poet's skull or whole body.

The Requiem by Verdi (another Italian) is a particularly
dramatic concert version of the Mass for the Dead; it
includes some immense drum-beats and sensational trumpet-
calls, the latter accompanying the part of the Latin text
which Raine includes here—'awesome trumpet pouring
sound through the bowels of the earth'. In anticipation of the
Latin text, and perhaps to help the inescapable onward drive
of this poem, Raine here uses rhyme.

A MARTIAN SENDS A POSTCARD HOME
Caxton was a pioneer printer of books.
Model T was an early mass-produced car.

FLOODS

When a boxer's support-team throw in the sponge, they concede defeat. The froth against the bridge *looks* like a sponge, and the bridge is defeated because it no longer links dry land.

Occam's razor is a philosophical maxim, which cuts out unnecessary hypotheses. The joke is perhaps mainly that the floods are in Oxford, where 'quibbles', 'digressions', and 'argument' are particularly frequent; Occam's razor might be seen as simplifying, as the floods cover all the 'points' (a pun here) of grass. It is a light-hearted poem.

IN THE MORTUARY

abacus: counting-machine using beads; so, beads of sweat.
terra cotta: baked earth (earthenware)—reddish brown.

LAYING A LAWN

tomes: heavy books. Lawn-turves are sold folded once, and are about the size and weight of very large art books. The weight is of course the layer of 'earth' which holds them together; but in 'Bound with earth to last' the poet is already preparing us for the premonitions of death later in the poem: earth to earth is dust to dust. The earth may make the grass *last*, but it is also what we shall come to at *last*—the submerged second meaning makes the first meaning bob about uneasily. The book idea continues in 'the simple text of grass', which in turn recalls one of the simplest and most well-known of all religious texts: 'all flesh is grass'. And it bobs up again, with great aptness, at the end in the *Domesday Book*—which was actually a catalogue of land (earth!) but which sounds like and makes us think of our day of 'doom'. The delicate firmness with which this apparently playful image underlies the poem (note that the very young child's books are at present 'wordless' and 'unread', as her life is as yet still mostly to come) is matched by the descriptive writing, which, as often in Raine, grips frankly and uncompromisingly on the fact of death, and at the same time delights in the detail of life.

Robert Wells

Robert Wells was born in 1947 and studied at Cambridge. He worked as a forester on Exmoor, as a teacher in Iran and Italy, and in publishing; and he now teaches English at Leicester University.

Wells's first book of poetry, THE WINTER'S TASK, was published in 1977 and almost all the poems in this selection come from it. The book reads particularly well as a whole—making anthology-selection less satisfactory—with a frequent overlap or back-reference of scene or form. Most of the poems deal with outdoor life, manual labour in traditional rural settings in England or Italy, and with the sense-experience and withdrawn, tentative emotional life of a young man (whom we may associate with the poet, though the third person is generally used). They are completed short poems, not fragments, but are certainly better for being read together, as an artist's sketches or water-colours may gain from being collected in one place.

Wells writes tersely, with the utmost respect for the language and verse of the past, of the main English poetic tradition. At times his choice of the classic English iambic pentameter—in, for example, the title-poem THE WINTER'S TASK—may seem to lead to stiltedness, but the poet may feel this a small risk to run for the corresponding gain in control and impersonality. He also values rhyme and half-rhyme, sometimes in quite discreet and subtle patterns which the alert reader can relish. This discretion and subtlety are also evident in content and in choice of words; a guiding principle has clearly been 'if in doubt, leave it out', and as a result some poems may seem tantalizingly obscure; but every poem is firm and worth attention.

Lost Company

Lost company, in the cold I ram each hand
Along my sides. Old warmth, a marsh bird's hoot,
A colour in the air, you fade. I stand
Watching farmers on patrol to shoot
The rats they bait with turnip root

Reset their traps at evening
And whistle to their dogs and go.
Winter is a black and white dog bounding
Over a camouflage of snow,
Ice sheets folding across the heave

Or sag of the tide. I fold
My hands under the folded sheet
To save them from the window's cold
And lie still, searching my own heat.
Snow fallen, all outside is mute.

Mist risen, all outside's a blur.
Lost company, if you could know
What drives me—I see the ground lie sure
In a pathless crust of cold, go
Head down in wonder at the tracks I leave.

The Changeling

The fruit falls in the garden where I played
And loaded branches of the pear tree stoop,
Throwing across my room a net of shade
Like old accomplices blackmailing hope.

Struggling amid the darkness to break clear
I waken from a field thudding behind,
My body bathed in hot springs of its fear
That rise unstinted from time out of mind,

And memory, like the seducer's hand,
Crawls in its trance toward the trapped events
Beyond the power of thought to understand,
Or hope, to settle in their final sense;

Where bending a stiff dazed regard at school
Beneath his daydream, and at nightfall laid
Between the new sheets, grateful for their cool,
The child was imperceptibly betrayed;

A stranger to the genius of his growth,
An image fastened like a fern in coal—
O doubt that catches in the breath of youth.
O muscle gritting round a spellbound soul,

Too deep within the luxury of its mood
To waken from the prayer to which it bends.
O mirage glittering in the waste of blood
Toward this thirst. O too sufficient ends.

The Winter's Task

The insects leave his toil. Frosts arrive
That starve the grass and bleach its paler growth.
Too thinly clothed amid the gathering cold
He works across the acres mute of change.
As the year falls back, he must yet persist
In the choice of effort, and outface till dusk
The weariness that forbids. The winter fields
About him spread their desert sympathy.

Standing by the white horse that nuzzles him
He touches the grey lips, to know what patience
Stables it out in light dark grass rain sun
And nothing kept, the stream run thin or full
That cloys and fumbles through the muddy field
And doles the pure fruit from its opened hand,
Presenting thirst, as air the breath, its gift
Derived in the same cold asperity.

For hand in hand with hope, life in his hands,
And clothed in powerful youth, he turns aside
From local ambition, even from the abyss
Of human feeling, though to stand at loss,
Frustrate or joyous amid the idle paths
Where nature cancels history, where strength
Of body is a means toward its own end;
And is the strongest he will ever be.

He lets his eyes fall on his folded arms,
Their yellow glint of hair, and tired his thought
Dwelling like sight heavily where it falls
And slow to move as he to lift his eyes.

He stirs at morning amid the ash of sleep
Light moving down an arm, moist shadow torn
Along the skin, the red, the white, the brown.
Dusk brings him ready to his food and sleep.

As each breath taken clears for strength a space
Of thirty seconds maybe to move free
And every movement hangs upon a breath,
He may think only of the next axe stroke.
Poor beggar of patience! The very thought
Reasoning his servitude discomfits it.
The end he labours for must seem the touch
Of sudden magic as he lifts his eyes.

His violence laid waste upon the hill,
His thirst extinguished in the lowly stream,
He conjures from a purified land at dusk
The hero's antique shrine; where at its hour
A bodily bright finished shape appears
And silent energies return, to offer
Their trophies rescued from inconsequence.
The cold increases. Darkness cheats the eyes

And he must come to himself, and long to break
The tryst of self-possession; setting his head
In the crook of his arm at night, and ignorant
What froze him at other times from company.
Then in the room his wakefulness becomes
A blank wall, shutting out the chosen scenes
Of memory, so that he lies in doubt
Whether the knowledge won begins or ends.

Imagined futures jerk his head from toil.
The bramble barbs that hook him back to lust,

And hope, a stray root withering in the air,
Melt nature's recalcitrance from his hands.
If the one constant is his own presence
Surely he labours toward his own defeat,
Creating only from the tempered land
A solitude askance amid the wild?

The stream set in its path, that runs more full
And gives suck to no trees; the chainsaw laid
Against the bark and drifting through the trunk,
Red and grey, chain black with oil, blue smoke;
Sycamore, blackthorn, willow mortified
To grey circles of ashes. When the task
Is finished, call it peace. Walls make a field.
Where saplings used to stand, the white stumps glare.

Daily his life wiped out, reduced each day
Toward this peace, the passive body sweet
And nature gentle in his mind, to live
By the blood's gradual renovating pulse—
It is not this youth is impatient for;
That labour so should neutralize its strength
Day upon day and year taken from year
Till darkness falls across a barren scree.

What part has patience here? What is content?
Less than a virtue; character broken down
Like leaves to soil, and as the spade turns up
The leaf's black imprint, so a man is found.
What end is the body? that he wakes remade
To quiet his heartbeat in a wider toil,
And all his being let go, that pulse through him
Leans toward the world still like a brimming depth.

His rest closes the day. When evening falls
All things attend upon his quietened sense
That keeps its watch, now self-possessed as they;
Distrusting sleep that comes without a name.
He wakes, as if such labour had not been,
Setting at break of day his hardened hands
And body's mastery to the one toil.
What can he keep from dusk but the one spoil?

Bonfire

The fire burns deepest at dusk.
He watches lively flame
Possess the waste, dry sticks,
Green wood with its crisp bark
And terrified sap,

But all the same in a few minutes,
From green to black
To white ash and the shy ember
Falling clear of it, and his return
At daybreak fresh with sleep.

His Thirst

It was the utmost of his thirst
To set his mouth against the stream,
Leaning his hands on the wet rocks.
It was his nearest to content
To feel the inward cold slip down
And quiet his body with its touch.

Love's Default

This is my youth in love's default
To loiter on the verge of day.
I watch the bonfire flare and melt,
The disparateness burn away.

The fluent heat wave leaps and churns
And scattered sparks are caught within.
Brief quick vitality! It burns
Two instants if it touches skin.

The Stream

Inopportune desire! It runs to waste
Too cold for love, too bold for secrecy
And falls from fresh to salt, an altered taste
Where grassy covert gives to barren sea.

Cattlemen

Dry sticks laid across
A piece of paper stained with oil
And a fire where we halt.
The sweat falls off and we drink
A mouthful of water and feel the cold.

The mule suddenly seems a lighter colour.
In the half dark
The fire paints strokes over the long muzzle
And flat hard forehead
And the forelegs

And the men move
Like more than men possessed
By their own lives,
Become what is evidenced by the rounded stones
Close in the path

And the rough stones lying like scree
At the side.
There are meetings here and things said
Though full light brings
Them back to themselves.

Breakfast

The pasture is a faded white.
Even the food palls
At the mountain's height by the spring,
A loaf in halves, unwrapped
From a blue cloth.
                              Oil and salt,
Raw ham. Sitting apart
To let the horses drink unscared
They brood what dream was broken
When mother or wife
Called them at four.

On the Hillside

I could not speak to him, but what we shared
Was the water drunk in the interval of toil,
The stream running over our wrists,
And I shared some biscuits with him that I had.
The water washed the crumbs about our mouths.

I could not speak to him. He was afraid of my glance
And jerked away from it to work harder
At throwing what I cut on the fire.
I was glad of his presence there on the hillside
Where the loneliness was mine and not to be shared.

Waterfall

Wet air and shadow. But the healer's touch?
The water on his shoulders fell like stones,
   Forcing his body to a crouch
As if to break through flesh and lay his bones

In the black pit of rocks. He crept aside,
An awkward stranger, from the water's hearth
   And felt returning as he dried
The worry that had brought him there to bathe.

After Haymaking

The last bale placed, he stretched out in the hay.
   Its warmth and his were one.
He watched the fields beneath the weakening day
And felt his skin still burning with the sun.

When it was dusk, he moved. Between his skin
   And clothes the sweat ran cold.
He trembled as he felt the air begin
To touch and touch for what it could not hold.

At the Well

The coldness of this water reaches beyond
Your worry. The look freshens in your eyes.

A hornet settles. Two rapt butterflies
Sip what you spill. The well-head burns your hand.

'Hardly Dwelt In'

Hardly dwelt in, always at risk
Brought by the touch of air at dusk
Or water in the mouth,

—And the drinker kneels, hands on the wet rocks
And the labourer stands,
His forehead crisp with chill—

Conviction that the body was not framed
To search in human task or love
The likeness of its need.

Virginity

Brittle, complete, and never something made,
No hard won recompense of casual harm,
It graced the body's peace and its alarm,
And glittered with the impulse that it stayed.

Fantasy

We would have trembled with the secrecy of the place
As if, thirsty, we could hear the noise of water
With nothing to hinder our kneeling there to drink;
And have walked, the bracken reaching above our
                                                    waists,
Some dog-rose petals cast large and white
Across the brittle remnant about our feet
Of last year's stems. Where the deer's hoof pushed at
                                                    the soil,
We would have lain, with only the sky to know.

Deus Loci

Imagine the embodiment of what drew you here,
A God standing on this mossed outcrop of rock.

He is on the edge of appearing, and is withheld
Only by so slight a thing as his absence.

Gran Sasso

Around the highest village, fields are ploughed
However pale the soil and frequent the stones.

Old habits huddle between old walls. The church bell,
Slight and unresonant, is a familiar sound.

Above the village, the final mountains lift.
Who climbs them feels his life thin out like air

And finds beyond the ridge a treeless meadow
Without a trace of history or occupation.

Then the summit, gross blunted rock that has shed
The last vestige of anything but itself.

Chinese Dish

If the shore is set with trees that can be named,
Among them a stilted terrace and a shrine,
It is to create of the white emptiness
A slow river, and to place there a fisherman
In whose contemplation this scene exists—although
His huddled figure, his boat tilting in the ripples,
His line are the incidentals of remoteness.

Shape of Air

It has lighted on you, this shape of air.
I don't want you to know that it is there:
Not yours or mine, as by the gate you stand
That divides the mountain from the worked land
And the first light of day, neither shade nor shine,
Shows through your open shirt your body's line.
The stones, the coppice, the inconsequent trees,
The cold fountain by the path, where blackberries
Rot on the bushes unpicked, and before noon
The cattlemen, work finished, will rest from the sun:
How casually you come here, bring that shape,
Stretch in the grass, drink from the metal cup
Its cramping mouthful; certainly of this place,
Your muscle-rumoured limbs and quiet face
And ready glee. O beat the earth at a joke
With open palm, it was the same smile broke
An age ago here, and the same shape lit.
The same hope as mine was effaced by it.

For Pasolini

Vecchio ragazzo di Casarsa, dear protagonist,
Where shall we find the like of your intelligence?
The hunters who come here on Sunday with their
                                    dogs and guns
Are not enough to keep the forest paths open.
Two years untrodden, and bramble will cover the
                                    track,
The broom lean across. They were paved once with
                                    stones
Packed in together to make rough and narrow
                                    highways,
Loosened now, a rubble, a watercourse, except
For some short stretches where the old work has held.
If someone climbs up between the crests of the ridge,
Pushing through bracken that drenches his boots and
                                    clothes,
He will guess perhaps that this was the charcoal-
                                    burners' place:
But who can imagine now what their lives were, find
                                    more
Than that if he scratches the surface of the mounded
                                    green
He turns up blacker earth—their trace? O early bodies
Moving amid the dark as it thins. O quiet voices.
When ignorant beauty chances to conjure back to life
The shape present in the air, who will be here to
                                    know it?

A Greeting

Small boy watching the pigs turned loose to root
In the rich grass that grows along the stream,
You greet me easily. What I hear in your voice
Is that the grass and water are as surely there
For you as for your animals. You are happy
In the sunset that picks out the hillside with shadow—

There is a fine intelligence in your eyes.
What I love is that it does not disturb
Your standing quietly among the things you know.

Notes

LOST COMPANY

The phrase 'lost company' is vocative: an absent person, identifiable only in fading sense-impressions ('Old warmth, a marsh bird's hoot,/A colour in the air'), is being addressed.

The poet does not tell us *what* drives him. But the final image sums up the mixture of bleakness and satisfaction he feels: in the pathless cold, the ground seems 'sure' and his tracks cause him 'wonder'.

THE CHANGELING

A changeling is a fairy or elfin child substituted in the cradle for a human one. The magic origins of the changeling bind him throughout this growth and perhaps stunt it.

The first three stanzas show the poet caught in dreams by childhood fears—summed up in the rugby-football image of 'a field thudding behind'. Even after waking he cannot fight free of them. These stanzas are an effective statement of a classic neurotic 'knot', which the images of 'net', 'break clear' and 'trance' confirm, and which is well caught in the curling word-tentacle of line 10—'Crawls in its *tra*nce toward the *tra*pped events'.

The second half of the poem is undeniably obscure. 'Where' in line 13 refers back to the 'trapped events' of stanza 3. The child's school daydream made him look 'stiff' and 'dazed'; his gratitude for cool new sheets at night suggests the 'hot springs of . . . fear' of stanza 2. Gradually the child's changeling nature became evident ('betrayed'). He was 'stranger' to the normal process of youth; instead he seemed fossilized. Doubt caught in his breath, his soul was 'spellbound' in a quasi-religious mind-lock ('prayer' and 'mirage glittering . . . Toward this thirst').

Wells comments: 'The poem is about the self-absorption of childhood becoming insufficient. The "thirst" is the thirst for a sense of existence, and the "mirage" is the false promise of reaching it by further withdrawing into oneself. The "waste of blood" is the body. The boy in the poem feels trapped, is trying to escape, and finds himself unable to. The next poem, THE WINTER'S TASK, is about breaking clear, laying hands on the world and reaching that sense of existence.' THE CHANGELING 'belongs to an adolescent feeling of dislocation'.

THE WINTER'S TASK
The subject-matter of the early poems in Wells's volume is a young man's voluntary isolation and self-searching: trying, as we often say, to gain 'a sense of identity'. (Wells's own note, quoted above, refers to a 'sense of existence'.) A poem not included in this selection uses the image of a knot ingrained in wood to represent an inner predisposition which is beyond any conscious intention. Another poem finds the poet striking with a pick, hour after hour, 'as if each blow/ Suddenly might find out for me the ease/Of the mind's movement.'

This title-poem is the longest and also the most traditional in manner, in the sonorous blank-verse lines, having the feel of an incantation, and in the 'heroic', slightly generalizing use of the third person. It is in fact, in the late 1970s, an exercise in the grand style: a developed rational consideration of the theme of self-research through toil.

Stanza 2. The fourth line means 'And nothing is kept, whether the stream runs thin or full.' The horse lives without memory, in the present, simply receiving the changes of weather or season which appear before it. The 'pure fruit' is, of course, water. The images of drinking cold water from a stream and of being touched by air (or, in this case, being given air to breathe) are recurrent and key images in Wells's poetry. Compare the 'thirst' in THE CHANGELING.

Stanza 3. 'though to stand at loss' means 'even though withdrawing from human feeling and confronting the natural world leaves him at a loss, not knowing how to proceed.'

Stanza 5 lines 5–6. As soon as he starts trying to reason out logically what binds him to physical toil, he becomes uneasy in that toil.

Stanza 6. To *conjure* is to call up from imagination or from supernatural forces. *Antique* means 'as in days of old'. The 'hero' is the imagined man by whom the land was first won and purified, who was in the ideal relationship with the land: now a god representing the human and the 'elemental' (Wells's word in a note) perfectly fused. Wells continues: 'The "energies" are "silent" because they have been quietened by labour. . . . The "trophies rescued from inconsequence" represent the world in its true existence which the senses, purified by labour, have been able to grasp, and gather into meaning.'

Stanza 7. THE CHANGELING is a help here. The labourer is determined to break out of 'self-possession', to put his memories behind him.

Stanza 8. The 'imagined futures' are a distraction from his attempt at pure encounter with nature (which melts in his hands at such distractions). But the second half of the stanza questions, as if on the reader's behalf, whether this single-minded devotion to the present toil is not self-defeating. And the rest of the poem develops this impasse: youth, in stanza 10, is 'impatient' for something further (more human) than this encounter with nature through toil, however ideal the encounter. In spite of the distant third-person tone, the poem reads like a personal statement from an unresolved position. Its slightly awkward heaviness and obscurity may reflect this. But I find it an important preparation for the more compressed and more colloquial poems which follow, where the poet's mind seems to have freed itself.

BONFIRE/HIS THIRST/LOVE'S DEFAULT/THE STREAM
Four poems set out as a quartet, where the first and third, and second and fourth, clearly go together. In the first two poems the experiences seem direct, vivid, almost brusque, and the verse is unrhymed (and in BONFIRE, unmetrical). In

the third and fourth poems the erotic feeling earlier implied is now explicit, and the forms are traditional, metrical, rhyming, chant-like, with some almost archaic diction. The resulting quartet is impressive in its restrained and balanced treatment of material young poets often make a mess of.

'In love's default' means where love is absent and missed. *Inopportune*: badly timed, unfortunate, misplaced.

WATERFALL

Many poems near this one in Wells's book describe bathing, stooping to wash in a pool, or simply drinking gladly. The relief is partly a matter of reducing personality or personal passion—'a sobered joy', 'the unbalancing dark, the water's touch' on a body 'that thirsts beyond the feel of its own grace'. In the present poem what might have been 'the healer's touch' is not so: there is a threat in the ferocity of the waterfall. Its 'hearth' has not been welcoming and he remains a 'stranger'.

AFTER HAYMAKING

In some respects, a companion piece to WATERFALL: the same number of lines, the same rhyme-scheme, and a similar verse-form (this time the short line is six syllables rather than eight and comes second rather than third in the stanza). Again Wells presents an image—the touch of air at dusk— which he uses on several other occasions. In a poem called AT THE PATHSIDE he writes: 'The touch of air that greets you as you walk home/. . . is the last grace to be won/Before dusk takes the world . . . Do not outstay the blood's heat.'

AT THE WELL

See the note above on WATERFALL. It is interesting that this time 'worry' is dispelled by the coldness of the running water. Note also the more or less metrical verse and the gentle *abba* rhyme, making shaped lines across which the short sentences are laid.

'HARDLY DWELT IN'

Compare the three previous poems in this selection. What is 'hardly dwelt in' is the 'conviction'; and the emphasis in the last lines is on the word 'human'.

VIRGINITY

stayed: prevented, held up. Virginity is bright with sexual attraction, but also compels respect.

FANTASY

A delicate love-dream. The verse moves with an easy openness. The image of thirst, and water 'with nothing to hinder' links with earlier poems in this selection.

DEUS LOCI

So vivid is the sense of being drawn to the place, so mysterious the experience of being there, that the metaphor of a God of the place (the Latin title) seems almost literal fact.

GRAN SASSO

Gran Sasso is an Italian mountain, high enough (over 3,000 metres) for the effects of 'thinner' air to be felt by the average climber. As one rises, evidence of humanity disappears and so finally does vegetation. The last line invites a parallel with the sixth line: the climber may also 'run aground on the dead fact of oneself' (Wells).

SHAPE OF AIR and FOR PASOLINI

Only the first of these poems was written in time to be included in Wells's book, but they illuminate each other. Pasolini was a leading Italian writer and film-director of the 1960s and 1970s; he was murdered in 1975. *Vecchio ragazzo di Casarsa* means 'ancient child of Casarsa' (the town of Pasolini's upbringing). 'Protagonist' implies that he was the leading figure anywhere he found himself—an outstanding man. Wells sees him as having been able to recognize the 'shape of air' of an ancient Mediterranean country life, where landscape, simple virtues, and a kind of personal beauty are united. Pasolini's work tried to keep open the paths, as it were, of that ancient landscape, amid the corruption and desolation of modern consumer prosperity. (Pasolini called the corruption *'La morte di pieta'*—the death of reverence. Wells's poem shows its own reverence for the man and his values.) The poem is also a literal description of actual paths in the Italian countryside.

In SHAPE OF AIR the poet himself experiences a moment of recognition—it is as if latent in the landscape is an ideal human beauty, which suddenly seems to appear in a particular person. The 'hope' in the last line is the instinctive hope one feels in what used to be called 'love at first sight'; but it is at once 'effaced' by the timelessness and ideal nature of the human beauty. (A slight overlap here with the ideas in VIRGINITY.) Wells comments: 'I hope that the contracted sense of this line reflects the contraction of feelings into one another that comes at such moments.'

Tom Paulin

Tom Paulin was born in England in 1949, but moved to Belfast at an early age and regards himself as Northern Irish. He was at Hull and Oxford Universities and is now a lecturer at Nottingham University. He has published two books of poetry.

Paulin writes little about himself. He studies, describes, and at times angrily challenges the world he sees: his writing has elements of fiction, politics, and the history of ideas. The imaginative sympathy for individuals which appears in a number of poems is never mushy, and becomes very tough indeed when translated into outcry against the environment (of human states, or of nature itself) in which they suffer. The title of Paulin's first book is A STATE OF JUSTICE; these are key-words, and others are *nature* and *history*. The seventeenth-century philosopher Hobbes, to whom Paulin has referred, saw states as necessary human collaborations against the bleakness of nature. But a state such as that of Northern Ireland is so reduced by the primitive force of vengeance ('every revenge is nature,/Always on time, like the waves') that it can be only 'a partial state' (the title of a poem not included here). 'Justice' is interpreted as vengeance, and the 'just state' (title of another poem) is one reduced to 'bare wood and limewashed bricks,/Institutional fixtures, uniforms,/The shadows of watchtowers on public squares,/A hemp noose over a greased trap.'

The poet may 'cry out/For a great change in nature'; but he can have no hope of such a change. 'History' is upon him—the word develops a frightening sharpness—and 'the process of history/Must scorn an emotion.' In the poem BEFORE HISTORY, in 'the long lulled pause/Before history happens,' we see the poet's spirit hunger 'for form', knowing that 'love' is 'distant'. The point about form is that a poem serves, as Paulin says in a long, manifesto-like poem THE OTHER VOICE, not included here, 'only the pure circle of itself'. The poem ends with a poet's dream of immortality: 'In the great dome of art ... I am free of history.' (The 'I' here is the spirit of the Russian poet Mandelstam.)

Form in Paulin is above all the excellence of the verse-line. Without generally using traditional metrical forms, he stays close to the feeling of metre, mostly having a regular stress-pattern; and the line-endings are not repeatedly at odds with the syntax. Again and again, the lines are fulfilled wholes in the way of classic poetry at its best; sometimes we are close to song; at a greater distance, but still more frequent, is a sense of the declamation or chant which were the origins of poetry. Such achieved verse (speak it aloud, learn it) and such toughness towards his subject-matter make Paulin feel a poet of particular integrity; I think no one has written better about the Northern Ireland of today, but it is not only as a local or topical poet that he deserves our attention.

Settlers

They cross from Glasgow to a black city
  Of gantries, mills and steeples. They begin to belong.
He manages the Iceworks, is an elder of the Kirk;
  She becomes, briefly, a cook in Carson's Army.
Some mornings, walking through the company gate,
  He touches the bonnet of a brown lorry.
It is warm. The men watch and say nothing.
  'Queer, how it runs off in the night,'
He says to McCullough, then climbs to his office.
  He stores a warm knowledge on his palm.

Nightlandings on the Antrim coast, the movement of
                                   guns
Now snug in their oiled paper below the floors
  Of sundry kirks and tabernacles in that county.

Under the Eyes

  Its retributions work like clockwork
  Along murdering miles of terrace-houses
  Where someone is saying, 'I am angry,
  I am frightened, I am justified.
  Every favour, I must repay with interest,
  Any slight against myself, the least slip,
  Must be balanced out by an exact revenge.'

The city is built on mud and wrath.
Its weather is predicted; its streetlamps
Light up in the glowering, crowded evenings.
Time-switches, ripped from them, are clamped
To sticks of sweet, sweating explosive.
All the machinery of a state
Is a set of scales that squeezes out blood.

Memory is just, too. A complete system
Nothing can surprise. The dead are recalled
From schoolroom afternoons, the hill quarries
Echoing blasts over the secured city;
Or, in a private house, a Judge
Shot in his hallway before his daughter
By a boy who shut his eyes as his hand tightened.

A rain of turds; a pair of eyes; the sky and tears.

From

You've made a table you say, and are happy.
It's easy to understand where you are.
I can see you in a room we both know,
Cutting fresh wood, looking up now and then
To a window autumn light comes through.
There is a green glass float on the sill
And two stone jars we found washed by storms
On the strand. In the blueness outside, frost
And a light that, touching, makes what you see.
In that still light and silence the long hills

That ring the bay are brittle, fixed in glaze.
The island below you is a lost place
That no one can cross to in the neap,
The winter season. The tides slack,
But they never pull back; the graveyard
And ruined chapel are not to be reached now.
A priest lived there in the house when processions
Used to cross the sands slowly, in black.
Rotting boards nailed to its windows, that hermitage
Is obsolete. The light stays at that end
Of the island, catches that small, broken settlement
Where thin stones, laid flat on a humped ground,
Are carved with turnip skulls and crude bones.
A soft grass covers them and light falls.

Cadaver Politic

The grey hills of that country fall away
   Like folds of skin. There are some mountains
                            somewhere
And public parks with metal fountains.
   Rains fall and then fogs freeze, drifting
Over empty stretches of water, forts
   With broken walls on small islands.
Rafted cities smoke in the rain and sharp posts
   Have been knocked deep into flabby ground,
Thin tatters of chicken wire strung to them.
   Coffins are moored in its bays and harbours.
A damp rag, it flies several flags—
   Bunting and boneyard streamers, the badges

Of territory. In the waste, silent valleys
  Clans are at their manœuvres.
At the bottom of a cliff, on a tussock
  Of ground by a lean-to shed, a group
Of men and women huddle, watching a man
  Who tries, with damp matches, to light a board
Washed on that coast by the grey sea.

A New Society

It's easy enough to regret them when they're gone.
Beds creaked on boards in the brick meadows
Somewhere above a tired earth no one had seen
Since Arkwright became a street name.

Their boxed rooms were papered with generations,
There were gas lamps, corner shops that smelt of
                                    wrapped bread,
Worn thresholds warmed by the sun and kids playing
                                    ball
Near the odd, black, Ford Popular.

Then they were empty like plague streets, their doors
                                    barred
And windows zinced. Dead lids weighted with coins,
Dead ends all of them when their families left.
Then broken terraces carried away in skips.

A man squints down a theodolite, others stretch white
                                    tapes

Over the humped soil or dig trenches that are like
                                    useful graves.
Diesel combusts as yellow bulldozers push earth
With their shields. Piledrivers thud on opened ground.

Just watching this—the laid-out streets, the mixers
Churning cement, the new bricks rising on their
                                    foundations—
Makes me want to believe in some undoctrinaire
Statement of what should be. A factual idealism.

A mummified Bentham should flourish in this soil
And unfold an order that's unaggressively civilian,
Where taps gush water into stainless sinks
And there's a smell of fresh paint in sunlit kitchens.

Where rats are destroyed and crawlies discouraged,
Where the Law is glimpsed on occasional traffic duties
And the streets are friendly with surprise recognitions.
Where, besides these, there's a visible water

That lets the sun dazzle on Bank Holidays, and where
                                    kids
Can paddle safely. There should be some grass, too,
And the chance of an unremarkable privacy,
A vegetable silence there for the taking.

Firelight

Framed among ornaments, one by one
you've started to become
the faces of dead people—those
who died young, who made nothing
happen outside us, and the old
seated in armchairs like thrones,
prepared to die, but smiling.

It closes in, like the evenings
silting the tall windows.
Your voices brimmed here, but now,
dead ones, I visit you with those
glances we know. Ask me how
we got to this firelight and I'll sing
in your voices, softly, of absences.

Before History

Mornings when I wake too early.
There is a dead light in the room.
Rain is falling through the darkness
And the yellow lamps of the city
Are flared smudges on the wet roads.
Everyone is sleeping. I envy them.
I lie in a curtained room.
The city is nowhere then.
Somewhere, in a dank *mitteleuropa*,
I have gone to ground in a hidden street.

This is the long lulled pause
Before history happens,
When the spirit hungers for form,
Knowing that love is as distant
As the guarded capital, knowing
That the tyranny of memories
And factual establishments
Has stretched to its breaking.

The Harbour in the Evening

The bereaved years, they've settled to this
Bay-windowed guest house by the harbour wall.
Each of us loved a man who died,
Then learnt how to be old and seem cheerful.
I think of being young, in the coastguard station.
Those cement cottages with the washing
Swaying in the sea wind. What can she see,
The girl I talk to? Victorian childhoods
Where little stick figures go flickering
Along the roads? Such eagerness that used to be.
A butcher's shop, a boarding house, the dead
Are smiling from the windows there.
So many names, faces, and used things.
Dry calico, the smell of cedar wood . . .
I keep them in a drowsy kind of wisdom.
I have my drawer of rings and photographs.

The waves rustle on the beach like starched silk.
And girls come walking down a staircase
Into a wide room where lamps are burning.
Love was a danger and then children.
At sunset, when I saw the white beacon
On the quay, I felt a tear starting.
But I was happy like a woman who opens a door
And hears music. It was your face I saw.
I heard your voice, its gentleness.
And I stared over the water at another coast,
An old woman in a sleep of voices.

Going in the Rain

An Adam house among tall trees
Whose glaucous shadows make the lawn
A still pool; bracken on the screes
Wedged above a lichened bawn;
A rectory on a broken coast . . .

Our journey notices these things
Which aid the sense of being lost
In a scoured countryside that clings
To idols someone else imagined.

Georgian architects, ironic
Deists, crossed over from the mainland
To build a culture brick by brick,
And graft their reason to a state
The rain is washing out of shape.

Atlantic Changelings

The breakers, the marram dunes,
A sea snipe beating over green water,
Footprints of passing visitors
On a curved strand . . . I trace them now
Like a hunched detective scowling
In a dead resort, and learn the gossip
Of a social summer—see this walled pit
Scooped by that peculiar child
No one invited to their sandy picnic.
See where Long walked his dog last evening
And where the professor's wife met him
By the tideline. They exchanged polite words
On its drift of dry shells, though a sea potato
In the likeness of a shaved pudendum
Splintered their good manners.

Far from their different societies
The scuffed patterns of these prints
Show everyone changed into transparent
Shadows meeting on this shore.
Their inquisitive uplifted faces
Challenge and beckon with a shy
Confidence, their soothed voices
Come floating from the class
I could belong to (like them I have left
The city to consume a wild landscape).
We will pack soon and the sly locals
Will repossess this expensive view.
In the windy now I hug my righteousness
Like a thermos flask. I cry out
For a great change in nature.

What is Fixed to Happen

We know it well, that territory.
It tastes of grit and burning diesel.
A banal sickness as the wheels turn.

The eye is such a cunning despot
We believe its wordless travelogues
And call them *History* or *Let It Happen*.

In those waterfalls of images
Each life is just a simple function
With blank features and one useful skill.

The rain glistens on thick monuments
To an age of lead. That state will fail
Because it must. Pulped bodies happen

In a charred street, and what we know
Is secular: imprisoned shadows
And black plastic shrouds. A public death.

In a scorched space, a broken nowhere,
A homeless grief beyond all grievance
Must suffer nature and be free.

It knows true pity is a rarer love
That asks for neither action nor revenge.
It wills nothing and serves nothing.

The Impossible Pictures

In this parable of vengeance
There is a grey newsreel
Being shown inside my head.

What happens is that Lenin's brother
(Aleksandr Ulyanov)
Is being led to execution.

He carries a small book
Wrapped in a piece of cloth.
Is it the Bible or a text

His brother will be forced to write?
He twists it in his hands.
I think he is frightened.

I am wrong, because suddenly
He strikes an officer on the face—
His gestures now are a jerking

Clockwork anachronism.
He is goosestepped to the scaffold.
The frozen yard of the prison

Is like this dawn of rain showers
And heavy lorries, a gull mewling
In its dream of the Atlantic.

Ah, I say, this is Ireland
And my own place, myself.
I see a Georgian rectory

Square in the salt winds
Above a broken coast,
And the sea-birds scattering

Their chill cries: I know
That every revenge is nature,
Always on time, like the waves.

The Garden of Self-Delight

In that garden to the south
the civil gods are ranged
like statues in a maze
of vines and bay leaves.

The fountain grows a dance
of dreaming surfaces—
none of my slow guesses
will tell how deep they are.

And the men who walk the paths
murmur and hold hands
for they are special friends
who like a fragrant verse.

The taut women pass them by,
virgins of the moon
drifting through the cool
evening in their gowns.

This is a playful place,
though I view it from a bruised
shore that is dark blue
and cold and rigorous.

How can I understand
these fine and gracious beings
who pass me by and sing
lightly to each other?

Saying art is for itself
and prays to mirrors in the sand,
its own mirrors of burnt sand
where the smooth forms look pure.

So tell me there's no law,
and all of life is like a wine
that settles and grows ripe
till it dances on the tongue.

A Lyric Afterwards

There was a taut dryness all that summer
and you sat each day in the hot garden
until those uniformed comedians
filled the street with their big white ambulance,
fetching you and bringing you back to me.

Far from the sea of ourselves we waited
and prayed for the tight blue silence to give.
In your absence I climbed to a square room
where there were dried flowers, folders of sonnets
and crossword puzzles: call them musical

snuffboxes or mannered anachronisms,
they were all too uselessly intricate,
caskets of the dead spirit. Their bitter
constraints and formal pleasures were a style
of being perfect in despair; they spoke

with the vicious trapped crying of a wren.
But that is changed now, and when I see you
walking by the river, a step from me,
there is this great kindness everywhere:
now in the grace of the world and always.

Notes

SETTLERS

Kirk: the Protestant Church in Ulster.

Carson's Army: an Ulster Protestant volunteer force.

This poem is an example, perhaps, of how dramatized documentary ought to be done: clear, vivid, the points crisply and briefly made. The title emphasizes the main point: that trouble is being *imported* into the troubled country. (These settlers will of course be very *unsettling*.) I find that the calm of the verse-movement conveys the sense of a situation working powerfully and blandly, which is unlikely to be easily changed.

UNDER THE EYES

Again clear and economical: a summing-up of the Ulster vicious circle in verse so crisp and firm that it feels definitive.

In stanza 2, it is 'scales' because of the obsessive notion that justice (traditionally represented with a set of scales) is giving as good as you get.

FROM

The point of the title seems to be 'this is where I am far from but would like to be.' The landscape used to be of human settlement; now it is only nature, here still and silent and in a way created by 'light'.

CADAVER POLITIC

The usual phrase is 'body politic', meaning the people of a nation. Here, they are the people of a corpse.

A NEW SOCIETY

Arkwright: an inventor who here symbolizes mass-production, for which the nineteenth-century terraced houses were built.

Bentham: nineteenth-century philosopher/planner, whose ideas are neatly anticipated in the previous phrase 'a factual idealism'.

FIRELIGHT

A gentler, lyric poem, in which song is suggested by the tendency to rhyme. The speaker speaks to those who used to inhabit the room. At the end he seems to be thinking of other places which *he* has left. Note, at the end, that he will sing 'in your voices'.

BEFORE HISTORY

Mitteleuropa: central Europe, where boundaries and nations have repeatedly been changed and insecurity is part of the people's history. The metaphor is of hiding like a spy or a refugee.

See the introductory notes on page 107.

THE HARBOUR IN THE EVENING

Paulin often sketches people in his poems, with insight and compassion. This Rembrandt-like portrait is of a coastguard's widow. The white beacon on the quay reminds her of her husband and gives her genuine happiness, unlike the 'seeming cheerful' which she practises usually.

GOING IN THE RAIN

The Adam brothers were distinguished eighteenth-century architects. The house is in Ireland, and exemplifies the English aristocracy's rule (or attempted rule) of the country.

glaucous: dull grey-green.

bawn: cattlefold.

Deists: men whose faith is based on reason. 'Ironic' to us, because they crossed over to build a culture better (more rational) than that of the mainland, but only managed a poor graft on to a misshapen state, and one unlucky in both its real and metaphorical weather.

ATLANTIC CHANGELINGS

The poet is dissatisfied with the middle-class 'changelings' who take possession, for their summer holidays, of this bit of wild Atlantic coast. He does not want to feel one of them, though in many ways he is, and he is probably sympathetic to the 'sly locals'. Something is wrong—class inequality? The separation of prosperous man from landscape? Perhaps everything is wrong: nature is wrong. But the poet is aware that his 'righteousness' is also consoling to him.

WHAT IS FIXED TO HAPPEN

Make sure you understand *banal*, *despot*, and *secular*. 'what we know/Is secular' because it is seen unemotionally as history, not, with a larger sense of values, as the lives and deaths of men. Compare the last few lines with UNDER THE EYES (page 109).

THE IMPOSSIBLE PICTURES

Aleksandr Ulyanov was considerably older than his brother Lenin, and his execution is sometimes felt to have stirred the young Lenin to political action. By such a view, a good deal of twentieth-century Russian history has been a matter of 'vengeance'. Apart from the general link with 'nature' at the end, there are hints of a personal predicament, of a poet feeling himself caught up in some revenge; but they are only hints.

THE GARDEN OF SELF-DELIGHT

A view, from a dour northern land, of the privileged world where art can be for art's sake. The view of this 'playful place' is ambivalent. Wine, however tasteful, *dulls* the perceptions; a society of 'no law' can become a ruthless jungle; and 'mirrors of burnt sand' seem like surrealist images of horror. On the other hand the 'dreaming surfaces' of the fountain's waters may lie over real depths; art *is* a kind of playing; and the trouble with the 'bruised' and 'rigorous' shore may be precisely its lack of song, dance, and good wine.

The part-rhymes in lines 2 and 3 of each verse give a faint song-like lilt.

A LYRIC AFTERWARDS
The poet's wife returns from hospital and restores his spirits. Paulin's calm verse-lines are at their best here.

Andrew Motion

Andrew Motion was born in 1952. He studied English at Oxford and is now a lecturer in English at Hull University. He has published one book of poetry, and a critical book on Edward Thomas.

In choosing Thomas to work on, Motion may have felt an affinity for his dark but firm writing about pain and defeat, and for its underplayed, apparently conversational manner. In Motion's case the pain and defeat are in others rather than in the presented personality of the poet. His book, THE PLEASURE STEAMERS, is in three sections, the first containing personal poems mostly addressed to a friend or a loved one, the second, INLAND, being a dramatic sequence about events in the seventeenth century ('dramatic' meaning not 'theatrical' or 'stirring' but 'spoken by an imagined character in a particular situation'), and the third section a sequence about his parents. Subsequent uncollected poems again deal with other people's lives, and particularly with those of people trapped—by exile, loneliness, illness, or (in the case of Anne Frank) by persecution. The theme of the trapped personality seems, in this open, quiet poetry, not an obsession but a generosity particularly focussed. There is an overlap with the territory of the short-story writer.

An overlap, too, with the language and movement of prose. Like those of many modern poets, all Motion's poems appear at a glance 'regular' but turn out to have no really fixed pattern. Each is in verse-paragraphs (one is reluctant to call them stanzas when they have no rhyme and no clear identity one from the next); each verse-paragraph has the same number of lines; and the lines look, and feel, roughly the same length—they tend to have a similar number of stresses. The sequence called INLAND does also use rhyme.

But on the whole there is little or no correspondence between the grouping and the movement of ideas—a good deal less, for example, than in Craig Raine or Tom Paulin. Poems such as the two ANNIVERSARIES printed here read excellently when written out as prose. Motion's poetry is thus a good place to study what does happen to 'prose' when it becomes 'verse'—or rather, how a poet who thinks (especially in the closing sections of his poems) in extended sentences is nevertheless also thinking in *lines*. Consider the ANNIVERSARIES, BEFORE COMPANY, or ANNE FRANK HUIS: study the gain in meaning, and in poise, by that faint hesitation which the end of a verse-line gives. The verse-paragraphs are less certainly effective; at least they make a poem seem easier to read (daylight on the page) and they assert that the appearance of pattern matters.

The effect is of control and sobriety—not cosy or song-like, but steady—suiting the realistic look at the circumstances of people for whom 'chances' (a key word) hardly exist. The quietness of the poetry seems that of an unusually assured young poet, working within himself, not having to prove anything about his 'brilliance', 'range', or, indeed, 'maturity'. Motion says he writes relatively little; one feels that the poems to come may be worthwhile and important.

Letter to an Exile

I

Today your letter with its usual banter of strangeness
—the forty years exile makes you write
'Napoli' now, without joking—until the postscript
'What would you say? Shall I come back?'

Was that unhurried? Or did you catch sight
over the quilted roofs of the steamer
returning here again? I know how it looks;
the rails freckled with figures who see

their wake scrawl itself out, and then,
beyond it, the hills reduced to mist
where they made their journeys, holidays,
abandoned attempts at a life.

These original, northern gravities!
Though it gave nothing, now England
renews its wide promises—the map,
hung in your room for sentiment,

daily becoming a landscape perfected
by absence; a locked island where riddles
abruptly solve; a spoor of rock
poised before the Atlantic.

II

Tonight I've come, as every night,
back to this lamp's blond pool, and here
is your letter again, weighed down,
repeating questions I cannot answer.

Other lamps hang in the city
through my window, changeable constellations,
lighting only the sleepless now,
the lonely listening for footsteps.

You say it was like that for you,
but you had visible danger—Spain waiting,
Europe waiting—and we have no sirens,
no wars, only a private, long progress

towards morning, without release
from what scarcely threatens us.
Look: their lights hold steady,
watching above the river; it uncoils

beyond my street, an oiled wire conducting
moonlight through derelict wharves,
and striking a swan's black foot,
arched underwater, swimming east.

But you know about water, how it assures us
of elsewhere—and if I could, I'd say
come here, and the river will fill
your return with chances. But time,

which you think heals, has broken
that promise. Now where the current
slides under bridges, it only brings
scraps from inland—boughs without leaves,

planks, grass, representative lives
dragged down as if England was emptied
by water. Here silence is not the silence
you want, to hear wheat stirred through

remembered fields, or a bird calling
from childhood, but the same, deliberate
ignorance, peering at history for comfort,
you left to escape; it's concealed,

but it's always here, even now,
as early risers whistle up side streets,
and others above them stumble through
curtained rooms, into first light.

Inside and Out

Two hundred miles from home I found
the one lonely room where you live,
and that, as you said, was 'Nothing,
really. Not even my own. See this?
It's Madame Dussart's funeral gown,
filling a whole drawer. Supposing
I died first, of boredom, what then?'

Then nothing again. A vacant room
where no one would see the sunlight
mark time in dust towards your bed.
As if we were ghosts of ourselves
we waited for darkness, watching it
deepen to bring us together again
like shadows, our close definition.

And shadows we stayed, or tried to,
knowing, before it fell, that night
after night would discover us still
caught in our absolute lives. If not
the room, what was there outside to blame,
hidden except when headlights below
reminded us where they travelled towards?

Vimy, Arras, Bapaume: I imagined
the brilliant signs, whitening south
through your country of maps and towns
in history. Nothing escaped itself—
not even the wind, tracing a ridge
of lost lines over the fields, always
raising the same delicate spray of graves.

They were complete societies, flickering
stones I knew by distant village names.
However I chose I remembered them,
all preserved no matter what deaths
succeeded them there, and us, who talking
each other to sleep at last heard only
their luminous silence we could not survive.

No News from the Old Country

I

Well, how do they look, the hills of Vermont,
now that you're back? Smaller? And closer the house?
In thirty years it isn't the weather that's changed them,
but you, contracting the past by turning away.

Restore it now. England's dependable winters
were never enough, but there, watching the hills
repeat their promise of danger, you're home
on original ground. Let it build back—

fresh shadows have pressed across your room,
and further, the forest you never explored
has flooded new valleys. O let it build back,
not as explicable, thin enchantment,

but as a place in extremity: all its rivers
and broken roads defining a wilderness
where you relearn your love of chances,
and, as I write, even by pushing out

through your gate towards the trees
to search for kindling, are suddenly lost
from sight in a flutter of snow from a bough,
and found in the dark, risking another world.

II

So it goes on; so I, in the old country,
live off borrowed adventures. Since you left here
nothing has changed to disturb its complacent stillness;
or rather, there's only your absence starting again

each day, unreal and substantial at once,
like a hole in the air. But otherwise
there are the same identical views, which never
develop or move: the park, the thicket of steeples,

and even the river which carries down news
from miles inland is frozen across.
The rubbish of summer sealed in ice!
So much for different worlds. Where are you now?

High up in the woods, alone? Here there's only
the city's floodlit, familiar dark
fading towards you as England turns out of the sun.
O love, how did it start, this suburban safety,

this living on rumours of action? And now,
when will it end, pretending a possible happiness
somewhere else, another beginning, a river
tapped at its first, immaculate source?

Inland
Part Two: Winter 1618–Spring 1619

Arrival

They came before dawn. Eddon, our neighbour, woke
                                                    us,
    his boots splashed through
the yard, dragging a dark trail to our room:
    'Come quick. They want you.'

The darkness bared its miracle, slowly.
    We stood leaning our hands
on the window, watching below us a gull
    slide into fluid land,

then farms marooned on their ridge, flash open
    shutters, and lights
jog up a lane, halting where water
    gleamed out of sight

to its distant sea. For miles inland
    a few hills, sluggish
and crested from froth, heaved up
    their crowns like fish.

'Quick. They want you.' I thought he meant flooding.
    When I turned back
I saw the strangers' boat ploughing the marsh,
    and grass foam in their track.

Sun flicked round the bay,
binding the outline of farms
to their reflections in grey
bands of light. The marsh
always survives. Always.

Cattle bunched in their shed,
uncoiling sweet wisps
of breath over my head;
fresh shadows spilt down
their flanks and spread

across water to flake
into shrinking fragments
over the strangers' wake.
Their boat put down
some men; one staked

its prow into our land,
waded towards us
over the grass, and
lifted one arm. Our world
dried on his hand.

An Ultimatum

I waited in silence, weighing a stone in my pocket,
    on our green beach;
a low boat swerved from the other's shadow
    and moored out of reach.

We saw nothing exactly; a stranger
    hunched in the stern
studied our silence, then stood. In the village
    behind us, quietly, locks turned.

Even his words were blurred by distance;
    we pressed to the shore,
thinking if this was the danger we feared,
    there must be more.

But as we stared at his elegant silhouette,
    into the sun,
we heard a tiny ripple of syllables claiming
    the village, then run

underwater over our fields until we were strangers
    in our own land,
watching our shadows circle on memories we could no
                         longer lose,

    or understand.

An Appeal Refused

In the church it was cold:
we knelt by the altar
waiting for fields to unfold
indoors the scent from flowers
of tamarisk, marsh marigold.

How could I leave that place?
I could imagine nothing except
its imperfect, stubborn grace
—but from the shadows
no saviour unveiled his face.

Did we want miracles? Signs?
I only saw light,
piercing the window, define
a forbidden landscape where
water and earth entwined.

We knelt until sunset burned
it to dark. Below us, as lamps
in the village returned,
out of the dark a thickening
silence smothered the love we earned.

Jesse Sease walked hunched, head weighed down
to take in the flat parish he lived for.
At noon on our last day, crossing the crown
of dry land, he stooped into his stone church

and knelt until evening, below his high shadow
hardening in the glass. When he came out
he walked to our yard: 'Go on up. I'll follow.'
One hand with its heavy ring picked at some cloth

on our cart; hens clucked through a dark door.
We could not meet his look, or anyone's,
but travelled inland towards our new law,
hoarding familiar, fragrant dust on boots and hair.

He must have stood by his church
watching our backs thinning in twilight,
then turned to the silver water, and lurched
in. We only heard our rough wheels grind uphill.

Searching next morning, we found him
drowned in the salty grass. He lay
with his head bending the water's rim,
the ring embedded in his swollen hand.

Anniversaries

The Third

Three years without sight,
speech, gesture, only
the shadow of clouds
shifting across your face

then blown a world away.
What sleep was that, which
light could never break?
What spellbound country

claimed you, forbidding you
even to wake for a kiss?
If it was death,
whose hands were those

warm in my own, and whose
astonishing word was it
that day when leaving
your sunlit room I heard

'Stay; stay', and watched
your eyes flick open once,
look, refuse to recognize
my own, and turn away?

The Fourth

The evening falls with snow
beginning again, halving
the trees into whiteness,
driving me with it towards

the end of another year.
What will it send for you
that this has abandoned?
You are your own survivor,

bringing me back the world
I knew, without the time
we lost; until I forget
whatever it cannot provide

I'll always arrive like this,
having no death to mourn,
but rather the life we share
nowhere beyond your room,

our love repeating itself
like snow I watch tonight,
which spins against my window
then vanishes into the dark.

Before Company

I

It is always the same: waking alone
to rows of ochre lights in the village
a field away, then watching them
flicker when birds set out or trees
drive shadows between. With no one

to listen I name them whatever I like
—say they are perfect communities,
windows restoring a hidden world
where happiness waits. Ten years
is little enough to learn their lives

ignore my own, enclosed in a tiny room
as soft familiar silence settles again.
How suddenly fear begins. Imagining
love denied its visible place. I see
him sleeping upstairs, who calls me

darling, his wife, and almost believe
the trust he gave has changed to dull
indifferent care. I have become
the sadness he never neglects, a death
inheriting all his rooms and turning

the lost society there to property
—tables and faded chairs which soon
others outside will own, drawing
their curtains apart today for views
of mist risen through freshening air.

There he is now, a footstep faint
in the bedroom reminding me how
I must appear for him—his dutiful
patient who will not recover herself.
Till then I am not even that, only

a ghost pursuing his every move
dependent on sounds. Room by room
I wait for water filling a bowl,
the click of locks, and curtains
drawn to find my fugitive life.

This is the one existence nothing
denies, the haunting which still
surprises him opening wide doors
on furniture blurred with dust,
and rubbing a window where lines

of stables stand in darkness below.
All he has lost surrounds him
mocking us both—a silent estate
of parodies I complete by lying
alone like this, watching the light

break slowly forward across my wall
until it defines me there in shadow
I never escape: immovable hands;
my hair; and always this listening
scarred face he cannot refuse or love.

Anne Frank Huis

Even now, after twice her lifetime of grief
and anger in the very place, whoever comes
to climb these narrow stairs, discovers how
the bookcase slides aside, then walks through
shadow into sunlit rooms, can never help

but break her secrecy again. Just listening
is a kind of guilt: the Westerkerk repeats
itself outside, as if all time worked round
towards her fear, and made each stroke die
down on guarded streets. Imagine it—

three years of whispering and loneliness
and plotting, day by day, the Allied line
in Europe with a yellow chalk. What hope
she had for ordinary love and interest
survives her here, displayed above the bed

as pictures of her family; some actors;
fashions chosen by Princess Elizabeth.
And those who stoop to see them find
not only patience missing its reward,
but one enduring wish for chances like

my own: to leave as simply as I do,
and walk where couples stroll at ease
up dusty tree-lined avenues, or watch
a silent barge come clear of bridges
settling their reflections in the blue canal.

Notes

LETTER TO AN EXILE

Section I. *quilted roofs*: an effective description of Italian tiled roofs, over which the steamer is seen.

spoor: track, remnant.

Section II. The 'exile' left England in the 1930s, when the Spanish Civil War and the Second World War were imminent. The exile imagines the young poet's England of today to be similarly tense and exciting. The point of this section is that it isn't like that.

Section III. In one respect, however, the England which the exile left in the 1930s and the England of today are the same: in 'the same, deliberate/ignorance, peering at history for comfort'. The poem is calm and matter-of-fact, but very disillusioned. The young speaker seems more realistic than the much older exile.

INSIDE AND OUT

The poet notes that 'Madame Dussart' is the landlady of the girl addressed in the poem.

The scene is northern France, the terrain of First World War battlefields and cemeteries. The incidental subsequent deaths, the incidental subsequent lives of the poet and his friend, are transitory by comparison with those 'complete societies'. There is little 'inside'; 'out', on the other hand, are the 'brilliant signs' and 'luminous silence' of names with significance.

NO NEWS FROM THE OLD COUNTRY

'The Old Country' is England. This is another letter, this time to a *former* exile from Vermont (north-eastern USA) who has now returned home from England. Again the poem is primarily a critique of England, which seems here 'complacent' in its mildness and safety: the severity of Vermont winters is a symbolic contrast.

The poem is well balanced between apparent casualness and an urgent unrest; and moves from colloquialism to unabashed traditional lyricism in the poetic vocative 'O' and the thrusting uplift of the last three lines. On the way there are several shrewd touches—the third and fourth lines of the poem; the contrast between 'explicable, thin enchantment' (the debased-romantic view of mountain country) and 'a place in extremity' (the original romanticism); and the image, early in section II, of 'your absence starting again/each day, unreal and substantial'.

The last five lines are fruitfully ambiguous: on the one hand, they follow naturally from the poem's remarks about England, as 'suburban safety'; on the other, they have a personal ring to them, preceded by no less than 'O love', and it may be that the pretence of 'a possible happiness/ somewhere else' is as questionable for the exile returning to Vermont as for the poet in the English city.

INLAND: Part Two

INLAND is a dramatic sequence in three parts, each containing five short poems all in four- or five-line stanzas with regular rhyme. The extract here is the complete middle part. There is also an introductory note by the poet, explaining that the sequence is about a village in the easily flooded fen country of Cambridgeshire, in the early seventeenth century, when the villagers were forced—by men who announced themselves to be the landowners—to quit these low-lying dwellings and move inland.

Part Two describes the arrival of the 'strangers' and the reluctant departure of the villagers. The deft, confident narrative, the lightly moving, easily rhyming verse, are impressive, particularly in the poise of the conclusions of each poem—the foaming grass of *Arrival*, the human lives drying on the stranger's hand in *Disembarkation*, the heavy ring—representing tradition, the accustomed life—inflexible on the corpse of the preacher, Jesse Sease, who chooses to die in the floods he has known all his life.

146

ANNIVERSARIES

Motion's book THE PLEASURE STEAMERS concludes with a group of poems about his mother, who spent her last years in hospital unconscious after a riding accident. Printed here are poems on the third and fourth anniversaries of the day of the accident. The writing is very simple; the ideas and the emotion, on the other hand, are relatively complex. The subject of the poems is not just the pathos of such a condition, but also the rare, weird tenderness and sense of relationship felt in the silent hospital room. Those who know Jon Silkin's poem DEATH OF A SON ('Something has ceased to come along with me') may find that it illuminates and is illuminated by these poems. The tenderness, and an indistinct feeling of child–mother courtship, are delicately touched on by the Sleeping Beauty comparison in *The Third*, and by the idea in *The Fourth* that the years since the accident are 'lost' time together.

In *The Fourth*, lines 11–13 mean 'until I choose (or am able) to forget the expectations I had of our (now thwarted) life together, I'll always be forced to visit you in this state of mind.'

BEFORE COMPANY

A projection into the mind of a woman ten years afflicted, in a way partly similar to that described in the ANNIVER-SARIES, but this time at home and conscious, though without speech or motion. The other face of the fear in section I is the pity (for her husband rather than herself) developed in section II.

In line 10 of section I we should understand the word 'that' after the word 'learn'.

I find the calm though baffled sentences masterly; the last ('All he has lost . . . he cannot refuse or love') wonderfully sums up the whole poem.

ANNE FRANK HUIS

The house in Amsterdam where the Frank family hid from

the Nazis in a secret apartment, and where Anne Frank wrote the diary which has become well known, is now a museum. The visit makes ordinary freedom seem rich, and full of 'chances'.

ACKNOWLEDGEMENTS

Acknowledgements are due to the following for permission to publish copyright material: Carcanet Press Limited for poems by C. H. Sisson from *In the Trojan Ditch: Collected Poems and Selected Translations* and *Anchises*; Carcanet Press Limited for poems by Andrew Waterman from *Over the Wall* and *From the Other Country*; Carcanet Press Limited for poems by Robert Wells from *The Winter's Task*; Carcanet Press Limited for poems by Andrew Motion from *The Pleasure Steamers*; Faber and Faber Limited for poems by Tom Paulin from *A State of Justice* and *The Strange Museum*; Andrew Waterman for 'Man Cycling Home in Donegal', 'Mother', 'A Butterfly' and 'Gardens'; Robert Wells for 'For Pasolini' and 'A Greeting'; Andrew Motion for 'Before Company' and 'Anne Frank Huis'. Poems from *The Onion, Memory* by Craig Raine, © Craig Raine 1978 and from *A Martian Sends a Postcard Home*, © Craig Raine 1979, are reprinted by permission of Oxford University Press.